Education and Care Away from Home

A REVIEW OF RESEARCH, POLICY AND PRACTICE

Moira Borland

Charlotte Pearson

Malcolm Hill

Kay Tisdall

and

Irene Bloomfield

Centre for the Child & Society
University of Glasgow

The Scottish Council for Research in Education

SCRE Publication 140
Using Research Series 19 (*formerly* Practitioner MiniPaper Series)

Series editors: Wynne Harlen
                   Rosemary Wake

Published 1998

ISBN 1 86003 043 2

Design and typesetting by SCRE Information Services.

Printed and bound in Great Britain for the Scottish Council for Research in Education, 15 St John Street, Edinburgh EH8 8JR, by Bell & Bain, 303 Burnfield Road, Thornliebank, Glasgow G46 7UQ.

Contents

page

1 Introduction 1
   Scope of the review 1
   Review format 4

2 Changing Frameworks of Responsibility for Children 5
   The key statutes 5
   Structural changes – evolving ideologies 6
      Decentralisation / centralisation 7
      The mixed economy of welfare 9
      Marketisation, consumerism and competition 10
      Children's rights 12
      Deinstitutionalisation and inclusion 13
   Linkages and comparisons between the legislation 14
      Collaboration 14
      Child or children 15
      The rights of children and parents 15
      Need: 'Children in need' and SENs 16
      Assessment 20
   Concluding thoughts 20
   Further information on the key legislation 22
      'Looked after' children 22
      'Children in Need' 23

3 Children Looked After Away From Home 25
   Legal status 26
   Length of time in care 26
   Age and types of placement 26
   Children with disabilities 28
   Why children are looked after away from home 28
   Shared characteristics 30
   Summary 30

4 The Significance of Schools 31
  School as a supportive service 31
  School problems precipitating care away from home 32
  Caring for children with residential schools 33
  School problems of children who come into care 34
    Non-attendance and behaviour problems 34
    Attendance outwith mainstream provision 35
    Children with disabilities 35
    Children who are educationally able 35
  The role of education in promoting resilience 36
  Summary 39

5 Educational Attainment 40
  Evidence from national cohort studies 40
  Attainment in foster care 42
  The OFSTED/SSI inspection 43
  Humberside study 43
  Leaving-care studies 44
  Summary 46

6 Educational Experience While Away From Home 47
  Policy and guidance on good practice 47
    Whole-school approaches 47
    Recommended systems and practices 48
  Educational arrangements 50
    Patterns of school and care careers 51
    Levels of exclusion and non-attendance 52
    Explanations of exclusion and non-attendance 54
  Mainstream schools: what young people say 56
    What is helpful from teachers? 58
    Positive school experience 59
  Mainstream schools and young people looked after 61
    Schooling on return home 62
  Specialist provision 64
    Types of specialist provision 64
    Effectiveness of specialist provision 64
    Looked after children in specialist provision 65
    Residential schools 66
    Education in secure accommodation 68
  Summary 69

7   The Care System and Its Impact on Education 71
Developments in child-care policy and practice 71
Social workers' attitudes and expectations 73
        The importance of education 73
        Expectations of children in care 74
        Social workers' understanding and knowledge of education 75
Continuity and discontinuity 76
        Moves of placement and school 76
        Continuity in education across the care continuum 77
Corporate parenting and effective links with schools 78
        Parents' contribution to schooling 78
        Personal interest and commitment 79
        Clarity about roles and effective contact with the school 79
        Responsibilities of foster carers and social workers 81
        Involving birth parents 81
        Parenting when children are excluded from school 82
Residential care and education 83
        The educational environment of residential units 85
        Suitable facilities for homework 85
        Staff's actions in promoting education 86
        School-related daily routine 87
        Culture and practice in relation to school non-attendance 88
        Training and educational background of residential staff 89
        Support services and integrated practice 90
Foster care 90
        The educational environment in foster care 90
Summary 92

8   Collaboration Between Social Work and Education 93
Policy and service development 94
        England and Wales 94
        The Scottish perspective 95
            South Lanarkshire: Educational Support Service for Children in
            Care 95
            The Inverclyde Children's Units Support Project 96
        Key elements of effective policy 98
Structures for collaboration 101
        Barriers to joint working 104
Collaboration in relation to individual children 106
        Care planning 106

Child-care reviews 106

Summary 107

9   Implications for Policy, Practice and Research 109

The educational situation of 'looked after' children 109

Implications for policy and practice 111

The wider context 113

    An issue for the 1990s? 113

    New attitudes towards children 114

    Consumerism and accountability 115

    Inclusion 115

    Partnership 116

    Priority to education and social exclusion 117

Missing from the research literature… 117

    Differentiation 118

    Longitudinal research 118

    Understanding processes from children's perspectives 119

    Understanding inter-professional processes 119

    Project evaluation 120

Concluding remarks 120

Appendix 121

Bibliography 133

Index 146

Acknowledgements

We are grateful to the Scottish Office Education and Industry Department and Social Work Services Group for funding this review and to John Tibbett from the Central Research Unit at the Scottish Office for his advice throughout. A number of people have helped ensure that this review reflects current research and practice. In particular, we would like to thank Margaret Johnstone, Gwynedd Lloyd and colleagues at Moray House for allowing us access to their work prior to publication and to Pat Cook and Meg Lindsay at the Centre for Residential Child Care for the use of their library.

Many staff in departments of social work and education across the country sent us helpful information about current policies and services. Some material referred specifically to the education of children who are looked after away from home and this has been included in the review. In addition we received details of other collaborative initiatives between education and social work which provided helpful background information. We are very grateful to all those who took the time to collate this information and forward it to us.

This review was initially conducted between January and March 1997 and updated in summer 1998.

We quickly learned that services are constantly developing and telephone conversations with some key people working in the field helped check out that our information was up to date. We are particularly grateful to Cath Colvin, John Toland and Francis Cooper in South Lanarkshire and to Jane Weir in Inverclyde.

1
Introduction

The commissioning of this literature review by the Scottish Office reflects increasing concern about how children in public care fare within the education system. There is considerable evidence that being looked after away from home constitutes an educational hazard, thus adding to the disadvantage which removal from home in itself entails.

Collaboration on this issue by the two key government departments, the Education and Industry Department and the Social Work Services Group, is significant in itself. Few commentators fail to conclude that bridging the gap between social work and education is a key element in improving educational opportunities for children looked after away from home. The timing of the review coincided with the introduction of the Children (Scotland) Act 1995. Reflecting the requirements of the United Nations Convention on the Rights of the Child, the new legislation incorporates the notion that all children are entitled to maximise their potential. Local authorities are charged with specific duties to ensure that the children in their care are not further disadvantaged and departments of education and social work share responsibilities for children in public care.

In common with the Children Act, which applies in England and Wales, the Scottish act introduces new terminology. Children are no longer 'in care' but 'looked after and living away from home'. This change is designed to encourage new attitudes to being 'in care': to discourage the tendency to view 'children in care ' as a discrete, often stigmatised group and to reflect that, in most instances, caring for children is undertaken to support and assist parents rather than take over from them. Since the review was written during a transitional stage, the old and new terminology are used interchangeably throughout. It should be noted that the term 'looked after' has a wider meaning in Scotland, where it includes children on home supervision, than in England and Wales, where it is confined to children placed away from home.

Scope of the review
The literature review was carried out over a ten-week period at the beginning of 1997. In addition to searching appropriate data-bases, we sought details of unpublished work through personal contacts with voluntary organisations,

project workers and academics working in this field. Information on developments in Scottish local authorities was obtained by writing to each director of education and director of social work (or equivalent). Prior to publication in 1998, some of this information was updated.

Geographically, we have confined the scope of this review to UK material. This was partly because of time restrictions but also because differences in the care and education systems make cross-country comparison unreliable. Indeed, much of the British material available relates to England & Wales which has significantly different legislation and contexts for both education and social work services. In Scotland, the Children's Hearing System is central to social work intervention with children and there are many quite distinct educational policies and terms (eg Standard Grades and Highers rather than GCSEs and A levels; 5–14 programme; no National Curriculum; little opting out; Records rather than Statements of Special Educational Needs). Partly in order to safeguard against unwarranted generalisation, chapter two provides a detailed discussion of the Scottish policy context. Where possible, we have sought to refer to Scottish material.

Recognition that the education of children in care is worthy of specific attention has been growing since the mid 1980s. Jackson (1987) makes the point that a computer search in 1983 revealed that not one book had been written on this topic in the English language. It was therefore not surprising to find that most of the relevant literature had been written in the last decade. Readers should be aware, however, that the research evidence is lacking in a number of important ways. Such research as there has been has tended to concentrate on professional perspectives. Very little has focused specifically on the views of children and young people (who have generally been treated as a homogeneous group) or their families. Practitioners as well as researchers should consider the areas highlighted on pages 117 to 120 of this book.

Emerging interest in the education of children in care can be traced in the Department of Health's influential 'research into practice' child-care series. The 1985 publication made no reference to education (DOH 1985), while a follow-up volume published in 1991 acknowledged that information on the education of children in care was thin and summarised the damming evidence which was beginning to emerge (DOH 1991). By 1996, when a similar but less extensive review focusing on social work services for teenagers was published, educational issues featured prominently (DOH 1996).

This review draws on various types of literature and information including

(1)   the few research studies which focus on the education of children in care, usually concentrating on attainment, explanations for poor performance and the nature of the school and care environment. These include studies carried out by independent researchers and in-house studies carried out by local authority staff.

(2) more general social work studies which examine education as part of research with a wider focus.

(3) educational research about related problems, eg exclusion, alternatives, non-attendance, schooling in specialist units and residential schools. This is potentially an extensive literature and we have selected the findings most relevant to children in care.

(4) reports and audits by Ofsted, Social Work Inspectorate (SSI), Social Work Services Group (SWSG), Her Majesty's Inspectorate of Schools (HMI), only one of which specifically focuses on the general education of looked after children (the Ofsted / SSI report in 1995).

(5) written information about local initiatives and services in Scotland.

(6) information / training materials for teachers, social workers and young people.

Six key works have made particularly strong contributions to the still limited empirical understanding of this area. Besides making frequent reference to these throughout the report, the Appendix provides short summaries of each. These are:

- Jane Aldgate, Anthony Heath & Matthew Colton – *The Educational Progress of Children in Foster Care*

- David Berridge, Isabelle Brodie, Patrick Ayre, David Barrett, Bernadette Henderson, Helen Wenman – *Hello – Is Anybody Listening? The Education of Young People in Residential Care*

- Felicity Fletcher-Campbell & Chris Hall – *Changing School? Changing People?*

- Felicity Fletcher-Campbell – *The Education of Children who are Looked After*

- Joe Francis, George Thomson, Sue Mills – *The Quality of the Educational Experience of Children in Care*

- Sonia Jackson – *Succeeding in Care – Residential Care and Education*

It is important to note that only one of the above (Francis *et al* 1995) was a Scottish study, and this was small-scale, with a sample of 27 children. A few larger-scale studies have been carried out wholly or partly in Scotland, notably by Kendrick (1995a) and Triseliotis *et al* (1995), but education was just one feature amongst many which they examined.

A final consideration is that changes in law, policy and practice *may* render some research findings obsolete. Such developments as the Children Act 1989 and Children (Scotland) Act 1995, as well as prominent reports like the Skinner Report, were intended to improve services for children and there have been significant innovations (for example as regards training and inspection in residential care). Recent research does tend to confirm many of the earlier concerns about the poor educational outcomes for young people looked after away from home, but there are signs also of increased, though still inadequate, attention to children's academic and other school-related needs.

Review format

In order to provide a more coherent account of the key issues, we have adopted a thematic approach, drawing on evidence on particular topics from across studies. Although the literature devoted specifically to this topic is limited, relevant information and concepts can be located in a wide range of research and writing about social work and education. Particular emphasis, where appropriate, is on Scottish-based material and the views of young people themselves. The result is a wide-ranging review which, we hope, addresses the key questions.

A strong message from the literature is that children in care do not constitute a clearly defined group in educational terms and that this has contributed to their marginalisation in terms of educational policy (Walker 1994). Equally, social work planning has accorded a low priority to educational needs. We begin by outlining in some detail the policy and legislative framework within which social work and education departments operate, identifying their statutory duties to children in care and potential tensions between these two major services.

Having set the scene, key topics are considered:

– the characteristics and circumstances of children in care
– the evidence that they underachieve at school
– ways in which the care and education systems impact on children's educational experience
– specialist education and residential schools
– collaboration between departments of social work and education, including examples of special initiatives or services.

In the final chapter, we summarise key points and identify some of the main factors which may promote or impede progress. Gaps in current knowledge and understanding are also highlighted.

2

Changing Frameworks of Responsibility for Children

This chapter starts with a brief review of the main legislation relevant to children in care. Beginning with local government reform, it then surveys the major structural changes affecting children's services. These include: decentralisation; the 'mixed economy of welfare'; the promotion of marketisation, 'consumer choice' and competition; children's rights; and deinstitutionalisation and integration/ inclusion. Certain of the basic principles behind the Children (Scotland) Act 1995 and the Education (Scotland) Act 1980 as amended are then explored, bringing out the policy issues that particularly affect the education of 'looked after' children. We end by reflecting on the new agenda since the Labour Government took office in May 1997.

The key statutes

The *Education (Scotland) Act 1980* as amended remains the legislative foundation for state education in Scotland: under it, education authorities have the duty to secure 'adequate and efficient provision of school education for their area' (Section 1). The *Children (Scotland) Act 1995* up-dates and largely replaces the Social Work (Scotland) Act 1968 for children, and moves away from relying solely on social work services to meet children's welfare – the local authority as a corporate body takes on such duties. Some of the key provisions relating to education and 'looked after' children are given at the end of the chapter.

   Other legislation and resulting policies have been important for local authority children's services. For example:

- The *Adoption (Scotland) Act 1978*, while amended by the Children (Scotland) Act 1995, continues to be the basic legislation for adoption.
- The *Schools Boards (Scotland) Act 1988* replaced school councils with school boards.
- The *Self-Governing Schools etc. (Scotland) Act 1989* allowed for schools to 'opt-out' of local authority control.
- The *Children Act 1989*, while largely applying only to England and Wales, introduced certain provisions for Scotland: eg those relating to regulation,

inspection and review of childminding, day-care and education services for children under eight.

Legislation that has been directed more at adults than children, still impacts on children's services, for instance:

- The *Disabled Persons (Services, Consultation and Representation) Act 1986* can require a 'Section 13' assessment for disabled children with records of special educational needs (SENs), as they reach school-leaving age.
- The *National Health Service and Community Care Act 1990* applies 'community care' to young disabled people aged 16 or over.
- The *Disability Discrimination Act 1995* largely omits primary and secondary education, but can indirectly impact on educational services (see discussion below) and certainly applies to other local authority services that children could or do use.

Of crucial importance, the *Local Government etc (Scotland) Act 1994* created 32 unitary authorities and radically changed the framework for local authority service provision.

Structural changes – evolving ideologies

On 1 April 1996, the two-tier system of Scottish local government reverted to a unitary system. Housing and recreation services were no longer separated from social work and education services; all became the responsibility of the new unitary authorities. Twenty-nine councils were created on mainland Scotland, with the three Island Councils continuing for Orkney, Shetland and the Western Isles. Mainland social work and education services, previously delivered by nine mainland Regional authorities, have in most cases become the responsibility of considerably smaller units.

As a result of the 1994 Act, local authorities are no longer required to have social work or education committees in their councils, nor are they required to appoint education or social work directors. Local authorities are required to retain a 'chief social work officer'. Some unitary local authorities have decided to combine departments, with several of the authorities joining together social work and housing. Fife Council has been quite unusual, in organising itself around strategies rather than traditional departments. Thus the 'Social Strategy' will largely take on responsibilities for children's services. Further amalgamations and restructuring have occurred in Scottish councils, as they continue to evolve after local government reorganisation. Powers are included in the 1994 Act for local authorities to work together to provide services, by means of either Joint Boards or Joint Committees. At least initially, local councils generally found such joint working politically distasteful, and such possibilities have not yet been fully exploited. Local councils have been more willing to engage in a purchasing role, paying for services from other councils, voluntary agencies or the independent sector (Kendrick *et al* 1996).

The changes in local authorities had a corresponding change in personnel and structures. Inter-agency collaboration between both individuals and services was often disrupted, with time needed to build up new working arrangements and, hopefully, relationships of trust and cooperation. Further, there has been a widespread panic about resources in local authorities. The Children (Scotland) Bill itself laid out a very minimalist, and arguably unrealistic, assessment of resources that would be needed to implement the final Act. Local authorities, facing drastic budget cuts and pressures from all sides, are working with the Children (Scotland) Act at a time of considerable financial crisis for many authorities (particularly urban authorities where there is more disadvantage). Many Scottish voluntary organisations have suffered financially as a fall-out of the reform, with some of the smaller ones disappearing altogether.

The boundaries of local authorities are not co-terminous with other state services, such as health boards or police. Thus, health boards may be dealing with more than one local authority in planning children's services, or inter-agency work for a disabled child; police could be working with several different authorities in areas such as child protection. Previously there were disagreements about services for children placed outwith a local authority and these are likely to increase with more smaller authorities. For example, if a child is placed in a residential school outwith his or her local authority, it may become a matter of dispute as to which local authority will provide and/or fund supportive recreational or social work services. While legislation does say that the 'home' local authority is responsible for providing for the child, these financial issues have long been problematic. The work undertaken by the Convention of Scottish Local Authorities will hopefully provide the basis for effective working agreements.

Decentralisation/ centralisation

Scotland will soon have a major form of decentralised decision-making, with the new Scottish Parliament. Beginning to legislate in January 2000, the Scottish Parliament will be responsible for a wide range of legislation directly and indirectly affecting children's services: eg, health, education and training, social work, housing, economic development and transport, and the law and home affairs (although neither social security nor employment). A new Commission was announced in January 1998 by the Secretary of State for Scotland to:

- consider how to build the most effective relations between local government and the Scottish Parliament and Scottish Executive so that collectively they can best serve Scotland's people
- consider how councils can best make themselves responsive and democratically accountable to the communities they serve *and*

- report to the First Minister of the Scottish Parliament as soon as possible after his or her election. In addition, the Commission may choose, or be asked, to submit an interim report to the Secretary of State for Scotland.

Taken together, the Parliament and the Commission provide a substantial opportunity to re-think the content and delivery of children's services, as well as the methods by which they are planned. For example, voluntary and statutory organisations (in the Scotland for Children Campaign) have joined together to lobby on the Scottish Bill, to ensure children's rights are central to the Scottish Parliament and that children's and young people's own voices are heard in its workings.

Local government reform is a form of decentralisation in itself – bringing decisions closer to 'the people'. Local authorities must plan for localisation even further, as the Local Government etc. (Scotland) Act 1994 required local authorities to prepare decentralisation schemes for their areas. Further, the 1994 Act firmly supports the continuation of community councils. The potential effects are not definitive for children's services; as with local government reform more generally, they are structural rather than policy changes. They could improve or worsen some of the issues raised above for local government: for example, equity in service provision; availability of support services; funding of voluntary organisations. Particular worries have been the match between decentralised decisions and local authority policies, and how 'unpopular' client groups will fare if community councils have more say in services. Such 'unpopular' client groups could be young people excluded from school or who have offended. On the other hand, decentralisation could encourage greater community participation and make services more flexible, accessible and accountable.

Devolved school management is a particular form of budget decentralisation that affects Scottish state schools. A minimum of 80% of school budgets should be devolved from local authorities to head teachers. Schools can choose their suppliers, but monies for services like special educational needs, psychological and learning support services remain centrally held by local authorities. Midwinter and McGarvey (1994) write that the real choice for head teachers will actually be limited. Local authorities will still determine centrally resources for new teaching staff, and managerial discretion will be minimal. Education professionals consulted by Kendrick *et al* (1996) felt confident that head teachers would continue to implement local authority policies. This is in sharp contrast to fears and, to some extent, experiences in England and Wales, where such decentralisation is more pronounced (Blyth & Milner 1993; Hadley & Wilkinson 1995). A particular concern has been schools' ability to select their students, which could mean their refusal to enrol children who might be expensive (in time or money) or reduce average academic results.

As decentralisation is promoted in some areas, greater centralisation is occurring in others. For example, Children's Reporters, who are key actors in the children's hearing system, are no longer local authority officials; they are now part of an independent national service (the Scottish Children's Reporters Administration). The centralisation trend can also be observed in education, particularly for England and Wales, as central government has taken on increased responsibilities for school curricula. In Scotland, changes in the curricula have been less prescriptive, but nevertheless substantial. Many schools are now working to the 5–14 curriculum, which respects the needs of all children to quality education.

On the other hand, adhering to the curriculum can lessen the flexibility teachers have to adapt to the needs of pupils, perhaps particularly those who have special educational needs or whose schooling has been disrupted. Progression through the curriculum is based on achieving standards, which counters other educational initiatives that promote records of students' successes and progress (Riddell 1996). More recently, a curriculum framework has been introduced for children in their pre-school year (Scottish Office 1997a) and new levels are being introduced to the curricula at secondary level (Scottish Office 1997b).

Scotland is due to have yet another revolution in education in the near future, with the introduction of Higher Still in 1999/2000. This revised curriculum will alter the curriculum of the last two years of schooling (aged 16-18), in recognition of the increasing number of students staying on past statutory leaving age and to cater for those less academically able. It seeks to ensure 'parity of esteem' between academic and vocational elements, bringing together courses taught in further education colleges as well as state schools. Vocationalism is also being encouraged by such new/ revised initiatives as Skill Seekers, Modern Apprenticeships and the New Deal.

The mixed economy of welfare

As the units of decision-making become smaller, so they may need to look outside themselves for service provision. This fits neatly into another concept promoted by the previous Government: 'the mixed economy of welfare', where services are made available by a variety of providers (Scottish Office 1994a). Local authorities, for example, were encouraged to become 'enabling authorities'. Instead of providing all the services themselves, they were to purchase services from others, including the voluntary and private sectors.

In social work services, this practice has been growing steadily in recent years. Several children's voluntary organisations have a long history of providing services in such areas as adoption, foster care and residential care. Residential and community-based children's services in Moray Council, for example, will be largely provided by NCH Action for Children Scotland and the Aberlour Child Care Trust (Mitchell 1997). Further education colleges are now independently managed from local authorities, and the careers service has been removed from local authority control. The 'mixed economy' can be found across a range of services affecting children.

The private sector has had a growing place in allowing local authorities to make capital developments, through the Private Finance Initiative. For example, councils such as Glasgow and Falkirk are proposing to use partnerships with the private sector, to enhance their educational provision (McCann 1997; McColm 1998). In pre-school education and day care, voluntary and private sectors have been key providers for some time. The consumerism of pre-school vouchers explicitly promoted non-statutory providers; with the abolition of the vouchers in 1998, local authorities have been identified as the facilitators of early years services working with the other sectors (Scottish Office 1997c). The private sector has voiced some concern that this may diminish their role (Chisholm 1998).

Marketisation, consumerism and competition

The 'purchaser-provider' split and the 'mixed economy of welfare' were specifically promoted to increase competition – and thus efficiency of service delivery, it was hoped. To address the lack of control consumers can have in public services, the Government developed a series of Citizen's Charters in the 1990s. These laid out the rights and standards for consumers, including the right to complain and to have effective redress. So, for example, parents have a Parent's Charter for education. Children entering local authority care are given a statement of their rights and responsibilities. Local authorities have also been required to set up complaints procedures.

Parental choice was introduced into Scottish state education with the Education (Scotland) Act 1981. Parents can request a school placement for their child, and the local authority has the duty to so place the child unless one of numerous reasons justifies not doing so. These factors include 'significant expenditure' and risks to 'order and discipline in the school'. Research on the impact of these provisions showed movement towards a two-tier system, as popular schools continued to improve and attract pupils whilst unpopular schools became 'sink' schools in 'sink' communities (Adler *et al* 1989). Children with special educational needs or who display unpopular behaviours may be most likely to have parental choice of school disregarded.

An overview of recent Scottish research on parental choice found that parents of higher social class and parents with higher levels of education were more likely to exercise choice, although choice has become more common amongst parents from working-class backgrounds. Middle-class parents are more likely to opt out of the state system and send their child to a private school.

The assumption that consumerism influences academic quality is questioned:

> Although the majority of the parents believed a good education was extremely important, issues of academic quality was not their main reason for rejecting or choosing a school. Mostly parents did not feel the need to examine all of the alternatives; rather, they wanted to find the nearest school with a strong disciplinary climate and a positive social atmosphere.
>
> (Willms 1997: 3)

To exert their power, consumers must have information. In education, school 'league tables' are published, covering such areas as non-attendance at school and examination results, so that parents have more information on schools. In March 1998, the Scottish Office announced changes in league tables. Each school will receive national benchmarking information, including provisional targets applicable to the school, which are calculated on the basis of comparing levels of performance with similar schools (defined by factors such as free school meals, relative attainment and performance) (Scottish Office 1998b). It remains to be seen what information will be made available to parents and the public at large (Nelson 1998).

The former Conservative Government also sought to increase the diversity of schools available to parents. State schools can 'opt-out' of local authority control, to become 'self-governing' schools. In Scotland, unlike England and Wales, very few schools have actually gone through such procedures (as of 1998). What has been more popular with parents (particularly in the Edinburgh area) is the means-tested Assisted Places Scheme (to be phased out under the present Government), where financial help is available so that children can attend independent schools. The pre-school education voucher was similarly advocated by the past Government as a means to promote consumer (parental) choice and power.

In these developments, children have been perceived as passive recipients of schooling, not as active consumers with rights of choice and influence. Choice of school lies with parents under education legislation, not with children. Parents have the right to appeal against decisions in relation to records of special educational needs, or their children's exclusion from school; children under age 16 do not have such rights. Children have no explicit right to education in law, which instead specifies the duties of the state (ie local authorities) to provide education and the duty of parents to ensure their children receive education. As will be discussed in greater detail below, the 'consumer' of welfare services under the Children (Scotland) Act 1995 is somewhat more balanced in recognising children's as well as parents' rights in decision-making. For example, older children routinely attend their care reviews, and have rights to have their views considered. Children who are 'looked after' are supposed to receive information on their rights and responsibilities as they enter local authority care (Social Work Inspectorate 1992). Next we outline recent developments with respect to children's rights which so far have had little impact on schools and the wider education system.

Children's rights

The UK government signed the United Nations (UN) Convention on the Rights of the Child in 1991, and thus committed itself to putting into operation the articles contained within the Convention. The preface to the Convention itself identifies three key principles:

- all rights guaranteed by the Convention must be available to all children without discrimination of any kind (Article 2)
- the best interests of the child must be a primary consideration in all actions concerning children (Article 3)
- children's views must be considered and taken into account in all matters affecting them (Article 12).

Other articles can then be divided into three areas: participation, protection and provision. (For a detailed analysis of the Convention, see Hill & Tisdall 1997; Veerman 1992.) Unlike some other countries (such as Belgium), UK ratification of international conventions does not automatically incorporate the conventions into UK law. The UN Convention thus has no legal force in the UK. The sole 'enforcement' is through the requirement of states to submit regular reports to the UN Committee on the Rights of the Child.

Nonetheless, the rhetorical power of the Convention is considerable and has been used to galvanise and facilitate new institutions, approaches and practices towards children in the UK. Organisations that are directed by children themselves (eg 'Article 12'), have been supported and (to some extent) funded. Children's rights officers have been established in many areas of the UK, usually to support children who are 'looked after' by local authorities. More and more concern is paid to listening to children's views (Article 12), and increasing attention to discrimination of certain groups of children (Article 2) in regards to culture, ethnic origin and disability for example. In its submission to the UN Committee on the Rights of the Child, the UK Government (1994) held up the Children Act 1989 in England and Wales as a key means of translating the Convention into policy and wrote of the forthcoming Children (Scotland) Act as the equivalent for Scotland.

While expressed in terms of children's rights, the UN Convention heavily emphasises children's rights to have their needs met. Far more of its articles deal with children's access to resources than to their civil liberties. In fact, it sometimes subordinates children's rights as social actors, to their welfare. The child's right to have his or her views given due regard is subject to others' judgement of their 'maturity', and some would say completely subservient to their 'best interests' (see Lücker-Babel 1995). Whether these welfare rights sit comfortably with participative rights is an issue open for debate (for example see Hill & Tisdall 1997; Marshall 1997).

In some quarters, the UN Convention is presented as an unassailable document, but it has also been subject to criticism. Certain requirements are much qualified by such phrases as 'when appropriate' or to the maximum extent of 'available resources'. It has been accused of being ethno- and gender-centric (Ennew 1995; Olsen 1992), particularly in its assumptions about families and parents. Despite having deficits, the Convention does bring together, in one document, a wide range of children's rights and sets standards that have been internationally agreed. As such, it has been used as a lode-stone for adults advocating children's rights in the UK.

The European Convention on Human Rights (ECHR) will be incorporated into UK law in 1998. Court cases taken under the ECHR to the European Court on Human Rights have promoted certain rights of children (eg stopping corporal punishment of children in state schools), but they have been the indirect results of supporting parental rights. Concern has been expressed that the ECHR is an adult-centred document with a narrower focus than the UN Convention, and thus may ultimately conflict with it (Children in Scotland 1998). On the other hand, the ECHR has always had a stronger enforcement mechanism which will intensify with its incorporation into UK law; it may thus provide a further means to ensure that children's rights are promoted and met.

Deinstitutionalisation and inclusion

'Deinstitutionalisation' is a term more commonly used for adult services, but its principles have also been applied to children's services for many years. For example, the use of residential care has radically decreased for children in Scotland during the last few decades. Instead, foster care is used or children are supported in their own homes. The Skinner Report (Social Work Inspectorate 1992) did state that residential care should be seen as a positive option and not a residual one, but recognised that foster and community care schemes addressed the needs of the largest proportion of young people and children needing care. There have also been attempts to make residential care itself less institutionalised by, for example, having smaller units located in ordinary family homes and avoiding practices such as bulk buying of food. Similarly, policies have been established to discharge children from long-stay hospitals if they are there unnecessarily (SWSG 1993).

One of the principles behind deinstitutionalisation is inclusion of people within their communities. The Children (Scotland) Act 1995, as discussed below, particularly promotes this with its duties to 'minimise the effects of the disability' for children and help them live 'as normal a life as possible'.

Thus, rather than being placed in specialist units automatically, children who are looked after and have a disability should, if appropriate, have access to foster or residential care in their local area. Several Regional councils had moved towards an educational policy of integration or inclusion in the late 1980s and 1990s. The Disability Discrimination Act 1995 was passed to meet demands for disabled people's civil rights. It requires a wide variety of services to be accessible for disabled people. As mentioned on page 6, the Act does not apply to primary or secondary education. It does apply to other local authority services. Services such as recreation and day-care, for example, may need to be fully accessible; schools may have to become more accessible as a result of disabled teachers or their premises being used out-of-hours for other services. Thus, while Scottish education does not have a specific obligation to promote inclusion in its legislation, there are several other pressures that promote 'mainstream' services for children affected by disabilities.

Linkages and comparisons between the legislation

While education and welfare services for children share certain structural and policy similarities, they are governed by different legislation. At times the legislation can be complimentary, but at other times it can be either overlapping or contradictory. (For further discussion of the Children (Scotland) Act and related legislation, see Tisdall 1997.)

Collaboration

One of the major challenges for local authority children's services will be the *corporate* definition of local authority, under the Children (Scotland) Act 1995. This is a sharp change from the Social Work (Scotland) Act 1968, where the duties on local authorities were predominantly delivered by social work departments. The new corporate responsibilities of local authorities are, to some extent, underlined by SWSG guidance (1997a-c) and SOEID guidance on assessing and recording for children with SENs (1996d). For example, when local authorities are required to prepare children's services plans, the chief executive is to take the overall responsibility (1997a). A children's hearing supervision requirement may specify educational services and then the relevant local authority would be required to implement it. When children have rights to have their views considered under the 1995 Act, this will apply across all local authority services.

Inter-agency collaboration is repeatedly emphasised in SWSG guidance surrounding the 1995 Act, as one its key principles. Of particular attention has been the new duty to assess children affected by a disability under the 1995 Act, which may have obvious cross-overs with assessments for Records of SENs. Also care plans and reviews developed by social workers for all children 'looked after' are expected to include input from teachers and education services (SWSG 1997b).

Child or children

The 1995 Act is predominantly written from an individualistic perspective. Rights and duties are generally expressed in terms of individual children: for example, with respect to a 'looked after' child, or a child affected by a disability. A key principle promoted by the SWSG (1993; 1997a) is the right of each child to be treated as an individual.

Education legislation, however, is less individualistic. For example, local authorities can refuse a parent's choice of school under grounds such as significant expenditure or the educational well-being of other students. The conflict between the needs of individual children and of children as a group has been highlighted by school exclusions: what does one do, for example, in the short-term with a child who is endangering others?

Because of the corporate definition of local authority, educational services will have increased duties towards individual children while retaining responsibilities for all children. So, for example, education services will have to take the welfare of a 'looked after' child as its paramount consideration in making decisions about that child (subject to the exception mentioned below). Education will thus have a heightened legal duty to attend to the needs of such children. At present, under SEN requirements, education authorities can find it difficult to reconcile the very expensive educational needs of one child with a limited educational budget for all children. They may find it even more difficult when a 'looked after' child's welfare is the paramount consideration.

The rights of children and parents

The 1995 Act is based on certain legal principles that address children's rights, to which local authorities must pay attention. For example, local authorities must, in relation to 'looked after' children: pay due regard to the children's views; help prepare the child for when they will not be 'looked after'; and give due regard to a child's religious persuasion, racial origin and cultural and linguistic background. (There are exceptions (Section 17 (5)), where a local authority can ignore its duties to a child if the public is judged at risk of 'serious harm'.) 'Children in need' services, discussed further below, must similarly be provided with due regard to children's religious persuasion etc. All these duties will now apply to local authority education services as well.

The SOEID guidance (1996) does recommend that children's and parents' views be included within assessment and recording. Such attention has been a matter of good practice for many years in education. But education legislation does not have such requirements to have regard to children's welfare nor their views; the 1995 Act means that educational services will be placed under such requirements, for certain children ie those 'looked after' or considered 'in need' by the local authority.

Parents also have rights under the 1995 Act, which will apply to educational services. For 'looked after' children, parents have the right to have their views considered when a local authority is making decisions about that child. Local authorities should promote personal relations and direct contact, on a regular basis, between a 'looked after' child and their parents. The new terminology 'looked after' was chosen to emphasise that local authorities should share responsibilities with parents.

Joint parenting is emphasised by the 1995 Act. Parents thus have a duty to consult others with parental responsibilities, when making a 'major decision' in relation to their parental responsibilities (Section 6). Court orders will seek to encourage joint parenting, through revised 'residence' and 'contact' orders (Section 11). Unmarried fathers can gain parental responsibilities through a simple legal agreement with mothers (Section 4). Educational services may need to consider to what extent they recognise and support joint parenting, particularly in situations where parents may not be in regular contact with each other nor the schools, nor even the child.

For children who are 'looked after', part of the difficulty may be in identifying who is taking on the role of the 'parent'. Local authority workers may need to see themselves as taking on particular parenting responsibilities: for example, for parental choice, in requesting an assessment for a Record of SEN, to appeal an exclusion or part of a Record. Education has increasingly become predicated on parental involvement in education. There are questions, then, in relation to who represents children who are 'looked after' in such forums as school boards. With the promotion of home-school agreements (SOEID 1998), who will be signing the contract on behalf of the 'home' for children who are 'looked after'?

Need: 'Children in need' and SENs

The 1995 Act imports a new category from the Children Act 1989 into Scottish children's services: 'children in need'. Children in need has a particular definition under the Act and local authorities have particular (corporate) duties towards 'children in need'. They also have particular duties towards children affected by disability, who are also 'children in need' (see the appendix) .

As can be seen by the legal definition, 'looked after' children are not specified as 'children in need'. The SWSG *guidance* does suggest that they be considered as children having needs (1997a), but guidance does not have the same legal standing as legislation. While local authorities must have regard to guidance, they do not have to follow it in individual cases. 'Special educational needs' has a particular definition under the Education (Scotland) Act 1980 as amended. Children have SENs if 'they have a learning difficulty which calls for provision for special educational needs to be made for them' (Section 1(5)(d)).

A learning difficulty is said to be present if children:

- have significantly greater difficulty in learning than the majority of those of their age; or
- suffer from a disability which either prevents or hinders them from making use of educational facilities of a kind generally provided for those of their age in schools managed by their education authority; or
- who are under the age of five years and, if provision for special educational needs were not made for them, are or would be likely, when over that age, to have a learning difficulty as defined above.

Education authorities must provide 'adequate and efficient' provision for *all* children, including those with SENs. Education authorities also must identify those children who have 'pronounced, specific or complex special educational needs which require continuing review' and must open and keep a Record of SENs for any such child who is found to have such needs, after assessment. Details are laid down in legislation in relation to parents' requests, appeals, assessments etc.

Legally, therefore, education authorities have the duty to meet the SENs of children, even if the children do not have Records. The Warnock Report (1978), which instigated the changes in special education, suggested that one in five children would have SENs at some time during their schooling. In fact, a small percentage of the total school population have Records in Scotland (1.9% in 1996 (Scottish Office 1996)). Indeed only around three-quarters of children in special (segregated) schools have a Record (Scottish Office 1996). The reality, however, is that children with Records have a stronger guarantee that services will be provided. Commentators in England and Wales have been particularly concerned about children with SENs who are not recorded (eg Hayden 1997; Sinclair *et al* 1994). With devolved school management, grant-maintained ('opted-out') schools and increased competition between schools, children without Statements (Records in Scotland) risk being expensive and hence unpopular students for schools. In Scotland, the greater risk may lie with cash-short, smaller local authorities after local government reform and budget cuts. Furthermore, other local authority duties (such as Future Needs Assessments (FNAs), for when a child reaches school-leaving age) are tied to a child having a Record of SENs. Again, it may be good and usual practice for all children in special schools to have FNAs but, without Records, there is no *right* to one.

Just as a 'looked after' child is not necessarily a 'child in need', nor is a child with 'special educational needs' necessarily a 'child in need' under the 1995 Act. The SWSG guidance does suggest that 'children with special needs', 'children with emotional, behavioural and mental health problems' and those whose 'educational development is suffering' be considered as children having needs (1997a). Once again, however, there will be considerable room for local authority discretion in determining who is a 'child in need'. Research from England and Wales (Aldgate & Tunstill 1995; Colton *et al* 1995b; Social Services Inspectorate 1994) indicates that local authorities have had problems reconciling their specific duties to children with disabilities, and their duties towards 'children in need' more generally. Local authorities have been confused about the fit between disabled children and 'children in need', and development of services has often been slow or simply not present.

A potential difference between 'in need', 'special educational needs' and 'looked after' lies in the location of the child's 'difficulty' or 'needs'. The 'looked after' definition is dependent on a child's individual situation. The 'in need' definition is determined by the child having a disability, or their health and development (as described on page 23). Both these definitions take a largely individualistic approach. In contrast, 'special educational needs' was at least originally intended to underline the interaction between the child's needs and the nature of schooling – and thus the school's responsibility to adapt (Warnock Report 1978). The Children (Scotland) Act 1995 could be characterised as locating a child's needs within the child, taking an individualistic approach, while the Education (Scotland) Act 1980 as amended could be said to locate a child's needs in the interaction between the child and his/ her schooling, a more social approach.

This distinction should not be too finely drawn. First, many have doubted that education has fulfilled its obligation to adapt, and SENs provision continues to locate the 'problem' in the individual child (eg, see Armstrong *et al* 1993; Fulcher 1989). Second, 'children in need' is a somewhat circular definition in that a child is 'in need' if local authority services would help them. An interaction between services and the child is thus established. Third, a child is 'in need' if they are adversely affected by a disability – which also relies on the relationship between a child and his/ her environment. None the less, the use of 'disability' within the 'children in need' category, when it is so studiously avoided in 'special educational needs', is noticeable, and the location of the 'problem' (and thus the responsibility for change and adaptation) is potentially different.

Research from England and Wales, which have worked with both categories for over eight years, suggests the difficulties agencies have working together because they have different conceptualisations of what is a 'child in need' (Audit Commission 1994). While making individual decisions, Colton *et al* (1995a) found that social workers were still struggling with a lack of specific guidance on how to define 'need'. Because of resource constraints, most managers interviewed by Colton *et al* (1995a) did not believe open-access, non-stigmatising 'children in need' services would survive. The only hope, as the managers saw it, lay in collaboration with the voluntary sector. On the flip side, social workers could face the dilemma of services that were provided being higher than community standards; some parents felt that bad behaviour was being rewarded, and siblings could be resentful or jealous.

As local authorities have the power to refine the definition of 'children in need' for their own areas, the definition provides considerable flexibility to meet local needs and demands. Scotland has even more flexibility than England and Wales, because far fewer services are specified for children in need. While Schedule 2 of the Children Act 1989 lays out numerous duties for local authorities to provide specific services, the 1995 Act only specifies ones for day-care, after-school care and holiday care. Such flexibility, though, has some disadvantages. Children might be eligible for a service in one area, but not in another. In 82 English local authorities surveyed in 1992, only 73% identified children in care as a predetermined 'children in need' group and 38% identified privately fostered children as one (Aldgate & Tunstill 1995). Given the smaller size of most local authorities in Scotland, migration between local authority areas may increase and local authorities with good services for particular needs (eg for children with disabilities, or young people who are homeless) may have increasing demands on their services.

Children's services plans were made mandatory in England and Wales in an attempt to address such difficulties in inter-agency working. Under the 1995 Act, Scottish local authorities have a duty to prepare, consult upon, review and publish children's services plans, the first due in April 1998. Research on English and Welsh planning experience has emerged (eg Aldgate & Tunstill 1996; SSI 1995, 1997; Sutton 1995). These found several gaps such as:

- unclear purpose and intention
- limited ascertainment of need, with some local authorities only assessing need based on past referrals
- limited data collection and analysis
- poor methods for determining priorities
- inter-agency collaboration and consultation sometimes lacking, particularly with regard to the voluntary sector and groups representing people from ethnic minorities. Without shared definitions of need, common databases, and agreed structures for collaboration, inter-agency collaboration was poor
- cursory consultation with service users and elected members
- insufficient attention to commissioning services
- lack of monitoring and evaluating outcomes
- failure to link with other plans and reviews.

Positive progress was noted, however, on improving cooperation across social services, housing, education and health, both in planning and service delivery (Aldgate & Tunstill 1995).

Assessment

Parents of a child affected by a disability can request an assessment, under the 1995 Act. Similarly, parents can request an assessment for a Record of Special Educational Needs. Guidance from both the SWSG (1997a) and the SOEID (1996) recommends co-ordination of such assessments to avoid unnecessary duplication for children and their families. A potentially confusing issue will be the different ages and legal requirements for assessments. For example, a child could receive an assessment under the 1995 Act up to the age of eighteen. Under community care legislation, a child can be assessed for social work services at age 16. A child with a record of special educational needs should receive a 'Section 13' assessment from social work, under the Disabled Persons (Services, Consultation and Representation) Act 1986. Children should receive a Future Needs Assessment, under education legislation, to look at opportunities post-school leaving age. Local authorities will need to sort through the various assessments required for older children, to ensure that the assessments meaningfully help young people access post-school opportunities and services.

The requirements for special educational needs assessments are far more stringent and specific in education legislation than are the 'welfare' assessments under the 1995 Act. For example, there is no specific appeal structure established in the 1995 Act, while there is within the 1980 Act as amended. Parents, or a young person, must be sent a copy of a completed Record; there is no such requirement laid out in the 1995 Act. The Social Work Services Group guidance (1997a) does make numerous suggestions in relation to assessments for children affected by disability that will hopefully encourage good practice.

Concluding thoughts

Children's services are operating in an environment much changed from a decade ago and likely to face still more change. They have been affected by local government reform, other decentralisation requirements, marketisation and the 'mixed economy of welfare'. Education, social work and other services are now required to work more closely together to fulfil requirements of corporate local authority responsibility. They must cooperate, yet their legal requirements are not always the same and are sometimes overlapping or conflicting. Education services will be in the odd position of paying attention to the rights of 'looked after' children – to their welfare, to their views, to their religion etc – which they do not have to do for other children.

Education legislation is presently out-of-step with the approach of the new Children (Scotland) Act 1995. On the other hand, all local authority services have the opportunity to work together in the best way to meet their obligations under the new legislation.

The Labour Government that took office in May 1997 has set in train policy initiatives that will affect children's services. The Scottish Office has appointed a Minister for Children's Issues and made a commitment to 'child-proofing' policy. Certain previous policies (eg pre-school vouchers and assisted places) are ending, and other trends are being re-directed (such as school partnership with parents and increased roles for local authorities in early years provision). Early years services have a raised profile (including a National Childcare Strategy). New monies have been put towards a range of programmes: for example, 'alternatives to excluding pupils from school' (£3 million), 'promoting positive discipline in Scottish schools' (£160,000), out-of-school hours learning projects (£23 million), an early intervention programme in reading, writing and numeracy (£20 million). The Government is strongly emphasising improvement in education standards (Scottish Office 1998b). There are also indications that the Scottish Office is considering setting education targets for children in care and may encourage local authorities to devote more attention to this issue in their Children's Services Plans (Henderson 1998).

The Government has announced its efforts to create a coordinated response to social exclusion; in Scotland, this has translated into a Social Exclusion Unit, the establishment of a Social Exclusion Network and a consultation paper (Scottish Office 1998c). Amongst the problems identified by the consultation paper are several that, directly and indirectly, affect young people who are 'looked after': school exclusions and other forms of non-attendance; inequalities in health, housing, and unemployment.

The 'New Deal' seeks to help young people (and single parents, those who are 'long-term' unemployed and disabled people) off social security and into training and eventually employment. As some of the potentially most vulnerable young people in society, young people who are 'looked after' may find their lives significantly affected by such policies as they develop.

Further information on the key legislation begins overleaf.

Further information on the key legislation

'Looked after' children

Section 17: Duty of local authority to 'looked after' child

'Looked after' replaces the terminology of 'in care'. 'Looked after' children are those under 18:

- who are 'accommodated' under Section 25
- who are subject to a supervision requirement (from a children's hearing or appeal from a children's hearing)
- for whom the local authority has responsibility because of orders made, or authorisations or warrants granted, under Chapters 2, 3, or 4 of Part II of the Act. These include child assessment orders, child protection orders, exclusion of alleged abusers orders, children's hearings warrants or authorisations, and parental responsibilities orders held by local authorities
- who are subject to orders elsewhere in the UK, which the Secretary of State has determined are parallel to orders in Part II of the Act.

Children who take refuge (Section 38) are *not* 'looked after' by a local authority. A local authority has a range of *duties* in regards to a 'looked after' child:

- to safeguard and promote the welfare of the child: the welfare of the child shall be the paramount concern
- to use services generally available to children, as the local authority considers 'reasonable'
- with consideration of the child's welfare, to promote regular contact between the child and any person with parental responsibilities to the child.
- to provide advice and assistance to prepare a child for no longer being 'looked after'
- before making any decision in relation to a child a local authority is 'looking after', or proposing to 'look after', as far as is practicable, a local authority *must* find out the views of:
  - the child
  - his/ her parents
  - other people with parental rights in relation to the child
  - any other person the local authority considers to be relevant.

  These views should be given due regard, as should the child's religious persuasion, racial origin, and cultural and linguist background.
- to review the child's case at regular intervals (Section 31).

There is one exception to a child's welfare being paramount (Section 17 (5)). When a local authority considers it necessary to protect members of the public from 'serious harm', a local authority does not have to follow the duties in Section 17. For example, a local authority would not have to give due regard to the views of relevant parties.

Section 29: After-Care

Unless satisfied that the young person does not need it, a local authority *must* provide advice, assistance and guidance to a young person:

- who has been 'looked after' at age 16 or after, but is no longer 'looked after'
  and
- who is less than 19 years.

On the application of the young person. A local authority *may* provide advice, assistance and guidance to a young person:

- who has been 'looked after' at age 16 or after, but is no longer 'looked after'
  and
- who is 19 years old or older, but less than 21 years old.

Assistance *can* be 'in kind' or cash.

A local authority *must* inform another local authority that a young person is preparing to reside in that other local authority, if the young person consents, either:

- when the young person is 16 years old and is no longer 'looked after'
  or
- when the young person is between 16 and 18 and is receiving advice, assistance or guidance, and has been previously been 'looked after' at age 16 or older.

Section 30 covers financial assistance towards the expenses of education and training, for young people who have been 'looked after'.

'Children in Need'

Section 22 and Section 93 (4)

Each local authority *must* provide a range and level of services to:

- safeguard and promote the welfare of children in its area who are 'in need'
- promote the upbringing of children 'in need' by their families.

Such services *can* be provided to the child, to the child's family or to a member of the family. Assistance *can* be 'in kind' or, in exceptional circumstances, in cash. The assistance *can* be free or families can be asked to repay, depending on their financial means.

A 'child' is under the age of 18, and 'in need' because:

- the child is unlikely to achieve or maintain, or to have the opportunity of achieving or maintaining, a reasonable standard of health and development unless services are provided
- the child's health or development is likely significantly to be impaired, or further impaired, unless services are provided
- the child is disabled
- the child is affected adversely by the disability of another family member.

A person is disabled if the person is 'chronically sick or disabled or suffers from mental disorder (within the meaning of the Mental Health (Scotland) Act 1984)' (Section 23 (2)), which is no change from the definition presently used. Specific provisions for children with and affected by disabilities are contained within Section 23.

In providing services for children 'in need', a local authority *must* have 'due regard to a child's religious persuasion, racial origin and cultural and linguistic background' as far as is practical.

Under Section 27, each local authority *must* provide day care for children 'in need' aged 5 or less, and after-school and holiday care for children 'in need'. Local authorities have a *power* to provide such care for other children.

Section 23: Children affected by disability
For children in its area, a local authority's services for 'children in need' *must* be designed:

- to minimise the effect of the disability on a disabled child
- to minimise the effect of the disability on a child adversely affected by the disability of another family member
- to give those children 'the opportunity to lead lives which are as normal as possible'.

A local authority *must* assess the needs of a child with or affected by a disability, when requested to do so by a child's parent or guardian, so that the local authority can provide the range and level of services required for 'children in need'. Other family members can also be assessed within this assessment.

For more detail on the Children (Scotland) Act 1995, see Tisdall, 1997.

3
Children Looked After Away from Home

Chapter two has provided the legislative and political framework within which 'education and care for children looked after and living away from home' is provided. This chapter is also an essential background to understanding specific aspects of the education/care interface and experience. In it we consider the characteristics and circumstances of four and a half thousand children who are in Scotland. We highlight their diversity yet illustrate that they also have certain common needs. One of the dangers of describing the characteristics of this group is that we may convey the impression of a static population which can be distinguished from other children. This would be a serious misrepresentation. Most young people looked after will spend most of their lives in their parents' care. Indeed the Children Act encourages the formation of care packages which may include periods at and away from home.

Children looked after away from home form a distinct group neither within the education system, nor within social work where they have much in common with 'children in need' and with those 'looked after' by virtue of being subject to a supervision requirement while living at home. Sinclair and colleagues suggest that a more helpful classification is to think of 'children in need' who at some points will be 'looked after' away from home. Based on a study of young people assessed for social work services, these researchers found that similar educational problems were present whether the young people were placed away from home or not (Sinclair *et al* 1995). Children affected by disability who are also placed away from home are children 'in need' before, during and after a period of being 'looked after'.

One of the challenges in developing appropriate practice in relation to the education of children looked after is to identify need sensitively, without stereotyping children or intrusively referring them to specialist services. Teachers interviewed by Berridge *et al* (1996) reported they found it difficult to think of children in residential care as a discrete group and frequently spoke of them alongside other children experiencing family or emotional problems. While this attitude is preferable to the automatic stigmatising reported by many children (Fletcher 1993), it will not necessarily help identify the needs of the academically able child who is having to cope with life in a new home and the differently ordered curriculum of a new school. Being looked after away from home creates additional educational needs for most young people but these will be as individual as the characteristics and circumstances of the children themselves (Fletcher 1998).

Unless stated otherwise, the information presented in this chapter is based on the latest published Scottish Office statistics (Scottish Office 1996 a&b) In relation to the total care population, the figures are for the year ending 31 March 1993, though the statistical information on residential care is available for the year ending 31 March 1995.

Legal status

Children can be looked after away from home under a range of legal arrangements. These include children who are:

- – 'accommodated' ie admitted to care on a voluntary basis
- – subject to supervision orders requiring residence away from home
- – removed from home on emergency orders
- – having regular respite
- – subject to parental responsibility orders, usually having been in care on a long-term basis.

Because there is considerable movement in and out of care, characteristics of 'admissions' differ in some respects from characteristics of those 'in care' at any one time, as the latter group includes a larger proportion of children looked after long-term. For example, almost two thirds of admissions are voluntary, but at any one time this applies to only about a third of children in care, most of the rest being subject to some kind of compulsory order.

Length of time in care

For many individual children, their experience of being looked after away from home will constitute a short episode in their lives. In the year ending 31 March 1993, approximately two thirds of children discharged from care had been looked after for less than three months and this applied whether their stay had been on a voluntary or statutory basis. At the opposite end of the spectrum, two in five foster children and almost a quarter of those in residential care had been looked after for three years or more.

Age and types of placement

In a study across three Scottish regions, Kendrick (1995a) reported that 28% of those admitted to care were of primary school age and 43% at the secondary stage. Just over half are teenagers. More than half of the looked after children in Scotland live with foster families, the remainder being in a form of residential care. There are approximately 2000 foster families in Scotland, spread somewhat unevenly across the country (Triseliotis et al 1998b). Foster care is the preferred option for younger children and approximately two thirds of those in foster care are under 12. Family placements can also benefit teenagers (Aldgate *et al* 1989) but since they are scarce, most older children find themselves in residential care (Triseliotis *et al* 1995).

The 1980s saw the development of so called 'professional' or 'specialist' fostering when a number of schemes were developed by local authorities and statutory agencies to encourage foster carers to look after older and more difficult children (Hazel 1981; Shaw & Hipgrave 1983; Hill *et al* 1994). Carers received specialised training and were paid a fee in addition to the usual fostering allowance. These services developed unevenly across different areas in Scotland and availability of placements for teenagers remains variable (Triseliotis *et al* 1995 and 1998). Fifteen year olds form the largest group of children in residential care. According to the latest Scottish Office figures, they account for 28% of the residential child-care population, followed by 14 year olds who constitute a further 19%. Only 10% of those in residential care are younger than 12. Boys make up 60% of the children in residential care.

Approximately three quarters of residential establishments are managed by local authorities, though a third of children are living in homes or schools run by voluntary or private organisations. In the main, homes in the independent sector are residential schools which care for larger numbers of children. The latest figures show that the majority of residential units are now quite small, although, with 6 to 25 resident children, still significantly larger than most family households. However a third of the looked after population were still living alongside twenty-five or more children. Occupancy rates in both the local authority and independent sectors were high at over 90% (Scottish Office, 1996a).

According to the most recent figures, the placement of children across residential establishments was as follows:

Local authority home	1020
Voluntary home	85
Residential school	602
Assessment centre	154
Special school	53
Hospital	8
Other, eg hostel	130
Total in residential provision	*2,052*

Kendrick (1995a) reported a variety of aims for residential and foster placements. Most were short term, eg assessment, emergency protection, respite, holding, or medium-term, eg treatment, education, preparation for long-term placement or preparation for independent living. One in seven had the aim of 'care and upbringing'. Residential establishments were more often used for treatment, education, assessment, preparation for independent living and short-term holding, while foster care was the more usual choice for care and upbringing, preparation for long-term placement, short-term child protection and respite.

Kendrick (1995a) and Triseliotis *et al* (1995) both reported limited choice of placement so that the preferred option was frequently not available. Even when the preferred *type* of placement is foster care and that can be provided, limited availability usually leaves little scope for ensuring that children are placed with the kind of family which is most suited to caring for them (Triseliotis *et al* 1998). Most children who are away from their family homes for more than a short period are likely to experience one or more change of placement, which usually entails a change of school too (Cleaver 1996).

Children with disabilities

Approximately 260 (5%) of children looked after away from home have a physical, learning or emotional disability (Scottish Office 1996). Despite this, we found no specific reference in the literature to the education of disabled children in care. In common with all children looked after, those with disabilities are approximately equally divided between foster and residential care. However more children with disabilities were living in residential homes managed by the voluntary sector rather than local authority homes. Of the disabled children in residential care, over 60 % had a learning disability.

Not included in the social work statistical returns are children with disabilities who live in residential schools but are not 'looked after'. Children with emotional and behavioural difficulties make up 70% of residents in independent special schools (SOEID 1996d). HM Inspectors now have responsibility to investigate how well schools meet the welfare needs of residential pupils.

Why children are looked after away from home

The situations which lead to children being looked after away from home are usually complex, combining personal, family and environmental stresses. Official figures do not reflect that complexity but indicate the 'main' reason as recorded when children are admitted to care.

The most recent figures (Scottish Office 1996a) indicate that during 1993 over half (55%) the children looked after on a *voluntary* basis were admitted because their parents were 'unable to cope'. Of those whose admission to care was compulsory (ie subject to a residential supervision requirement), the main grounds of referral were as follows:

beyond parental control	38%
truancy	28%
lack of parental care	17%
offending	9%

The number of children coming into care on truancy grounds has fallen, but they continue to constitute a substantial proportion of statutory admissions. Under the Children (Scotland) Act 1995, school non-attendance remains a ground for referral to the Children's Panel and, in contrast with England and Wales, any supervision disposals which may result are carried out primarily by social work rather than education services.

A number of studies which have looked in more detail at the circumstances of children's admissions to care have pointed out that reasons for care are usually more complex than official classifications imply. Several problems often combine and there is an element of arbitrariness in how particular situations are viewed. Kendrick (1995a), for example, pointed out that a child might have been in care originally because of abuse or neglect but be readmitted because of behaviour problems or as outwith control.

A key distinction for many children in care is whether or not they are 'responsible' for their entry to care on account of their own behaviour. Some researchers have also tried to make this distinction. For instance, Packman and colleagues (1986) coined the term 'villains' to characterise those with offending or behaviour problems, as opposed to 'victims' (of abuse or poor care) and 'volunteers' (admitted on grounds of family difficulties). Similarly, Farmer and Parker (1991) distinguished between 'protected' and 'disaffected' groups of children.

In their study of teenagers in receipt of social work services, Triseliotis *et al* (1995) were unable to develop such a clear classification since the difficulties of the 116 young people who took part in their study were inextricably linked. The main difficulties thought to have precipitated entry to care were as follows:

home / family-based problems	45%
behaviour in the community, including offending and drug use	39%
school problems, including non-attendance	16%

Although these were the main difficulties, they seldom existed in isolation. Though few teenagers had come into care directly because of abuse or neglect, these were features of many of their lives. At least one family-based problem existed for four out of five young people admitted to care and family circumstances were fraught and unreliable for many of the young people whose admission to care was primarily because of offending or truancy. Similarly, offending, school non-attendance or misbehaviour in school exacerbated difficulties at home and contributed to some parents feeling they could no longer cope. However one looks at the figures, it is clear that the majority of young people looked after are more 'sinned against' than 'sinning', a fact which, young people tell us, is too often misunderstood (Bullock *et al* 1993; Fletcher 1993).

Shared characteristics

Though children looked after are a diverse group with individual needs and wishes, there is also evidence that they share some important characteristics. Bebbington and Miles (1989) demonstrated that children who are socially disadvantaged are much more likely to become looked after than children with average or better social and material circumstances. In a study of 2,500 children admitted to care, these researchers found that, before admission:

– only a quarter were living with both parents
– almost three quarters of their families received income support
– only one in five lived in owner-occupied housing
– over half were living in poor neighbourhoods.

Children in care also share the experience of moving away from home and the disruption and emotional trauma which this usually entails. Often this impacts on their capacity to learn so that additional educational support is required (Biehal *et al* 1995; Ofsted / SSI 1995).

The local authority has specific duties towards all looked after children, notably to safeguard and promote their welfare, to prepare them for when they are no longer looked after and to ensure they have access to services used by children living with their own families. Maximising their educational opportunity is evidently a crucial element in equipping young people for life beyond care.

Summary

Children who become looked after are a diverse group in terms of age, the length of time they spend away from home and the type of placement they live in during that time. Around 5% have a specific disability. They are also looked after for different reasons, though family problems are common and the majority are disadvantaged in terms of social and material circumstances. Under the Children (Scotland) Act 1995, local authorities have several specific duties towards children in their care. Maximising educational opportunity is an integral component of fulfilling these responsibilities.

4

The Significance of Schools

In the previous chapter the main reasons why children become looked after were outlined, recognising that for each child this outcome is the result of a complex interaction between personal characteristics, behaviour and family circumstances. Another important factor is the availability of support services, including education. In this chapter we consider the ways in which schools and other educational services may influence decisions about children's care. We begin by outlining the potential significance of the school's response to difficulties then elaborate on the scale and nature of school problems among young people prior to being admitted to care.

One of the most salient points to emerge from the literature on this subject is that the structural separation of social work and education services is completely at odds with children's experience. Being taught and being cared for, whether at home or elsewhere, are closely interlinked aspects of children's lives. The quality of care the child receives at home has an impact on behaviour and performance in school while school can help alleviate or aggravate any home-based problems. Parker (1980) argued strongly that reducing the distinctions between education and care is ultimately in the best interests of children: 'Some of the best care can assume an educational form; and some of the best education and efficient learning can be attained in what is narrowly regarded as a 'care' setting'. In chapter eight, we focus on collaboration between social work and education departments in relation to policy and structural systems. Here our focus is on some of the ways school and care issues come together in children's lives.

School as a supportive service

Parker (1980) pointed out that attendance at school is a major support to children and parents and as such helps sustain care arrangements for children in their own homes: 'There is a sense in which education offers substitute care to all children providing, as it does during the day, a safe environment, food and a wide spectrum of rewarding and challenging activities'. He argued that schools are a key resource in keeping children within their families and that ordinary and special schools have increasingly seen it as part of their work to provide compensatory experience for children who appear to have had insufficient care during their early years. Indeed some children who have an alcoholic parent have indicated to researchers that focusing on school is one way of coping with an adverse home situation (Laybourn *et al* 1996).

Schools' responses to non-attendance and to integrating children with special needs will significantly influence which children go away from home and teachers' reports become a powerful part of the evidence on which decisions about children's futures will be made (Parker 1980). Based on a survey of children admitted to care from December 1994 to August 1995, an in-house study carried out in Fife (Ramsey 1995) suggested that variations amongst individual schools in their responses to difficult behaviour had a bearing on whether children came into care or not. In 58% of compulsory admissions there had been complaints about the child's behaviour in school. This rose to 72% when children were 12 or older. The proportion was higher in some areas than others which led the author to hypothesise that school regime and attitudes influenced decisions about removal from home.

In a Scottish study of children who came into care, Kendrick (1995a) also found that school support influenced how the care episode progressed. He illustrates this with the following quotations from social workers:

> 'Education was significant in that [High School] stuck with the child. They could quite easily have given up on him. They adopted a flexible approach which was helpful and they were prepared to negotiate. They took him back into the school system each time he went off, so he did not feel he was not part of [High School].'

> 'The school gave up on her very quickly. They were not interested in looking at the issues of alcohol and drug abuse. They were only concerned about her lack of attendance. She left prematurely without getting any qualifications.'

In their study of children returning home after being looked after, Bullock *et al* (1993) argued that integration back into the school was a major issue, especially for teenagers. Schools which appreciated that this is a difficult process and provided a sympathetic teacher for support made an important contribution to the success or failure of the return home.

School problems precipitating care away from home

The potential for school problems to lead to care has been widely recognised and since the 1980s most Scottish authorities have sought to reduce this (Strathclyde 1988; Kendrick 1995b). Joint policies between departments of social work and education were developed, based on early warning and collaboration, provision of a range of alternative services and effective gate-keeping to prevent young people moving too quickly through the system. Most operated primarily on a 'case' basis, involving joint planning amongst a range of relevant professionals for children with identified difficulties, though some adopted a community development approach with provision for all young people of school age (Kendrick 1995b).

Scottish Office statistics show the number of children coming into care directly because of school problems has been dropping but truancy still accounted for over a quarter of residential supervision requirements made by the Children's Panels in the year ending 31 March 1993 (Scottish Office 1996a). In our own small survey, responses from several social work managers indicated that reducing the number of children admitted to care for school-related problems continues to be an important objective in some authorities.

It has been argued that this emphasis on keeping children out of care or specialist provision has reduced the educational opportunities for some children. Panel members in Kendrick's study complained that problems of school attendance were often entrenched by the time children came to their attention and staff in residential schools shared these frustrations, saying that they began working with children too late in their school careers. Triseliotis and colleagues (1995) also found that gate-keeping procedures resulted in some young people having little education until their last school year. This was strongly criticised by some parents who said they had known from the start that alternative educational arrangements were needed. Their comments echo concerns expressed by HMI Inspectors that failure to take radical steps at an early stage might expose the child to repeated failure in unsuitable alternative provisions (HMI Inspector of Schools 1990).

Sinclair *et al* (1995) make the point that school-related problems contribute to the need to admit to care in both direct and indirect ways. In their study of 75 adolescents referred for assessment in a London borough, they found that not dealing with school problems at an early stage increased the likelihood that young people would become 'looked after'. Unresolved school problems had the potential to fuel other difficulties at home or in the community. Triseliotis *et al* (1995) also reported that non-attendance or school-based problems increased pressures within the family which then directly resulted in the child leaving home.

Caring for children within residential schools

The co-existence of school and other problems raises the possibility that children may be enrolled in a residential school, ostensibly for educational reasons, although other problems are equally pressing. In contrast with foster care and residential units, this form of placement combines care and education in the same place.

Secondary analysis by Loughran *et al* (1992) of the Office of Population, Censuses and Surveys (SPCS) data on children with disabilities living in communal establishments highlighted the apparent use of residential schools for all-year care rather than for special education. This has been attributed to parents being unwilling to acknowledge the need for a substitute family. The Skinner report (Scottish Office 1992) recognised that there is inadequate provision for children with disabilities and encouraged local authorities and health boards to develop their plans for specialised residential or family provision, as an alternative to hospital care.

Where homes are closed, some children may go to schools for 'care' reasons. When one English social services department (Warwickshire) closed down its children's homes, the number of children cared for in residential schools managed by the education department increased (Cliffe & Berridge 1991). A similar increase in the use of residential schools was noted in Manchester following closure of their homes with in-house educational provision (Rea-Price & Pugh 1996).

The interrelatedness of schooling and care in providing for children 'in need' is thus clear and which route children take may depend as much on local practice and provision as on individual needs.

School problems of children who come into care

Many of those who come into care already have established educational problems in terms of non-attendance, behaviour in school and/or attainment. This is not surprising, given their prior experiences of deprivation, the disruption in their lives and the fact that school difficulties often contribute to admission to care. As noted by Aldgate (1990), little data has been collated about children's attainment before being looked after but non-attendance and behaviour problems will have hampered academic progress in many instances.

Non-attendance and behaviour problems

Almost half the 200 children whose progress in care was charted by Kendrick (1995a) had problems of non-attendance at school before coming into care. This applied to more than three quarters of the 36 young people remaining in mainstream school, who were admitted to care for offending or behaviour problems. Perhaps more surprisingly, almost a third of the 38 child-protection cases had also truanted before coming into care. Thus non-attendance accompanied family, as well as behaviour, problems.

A Fife in-house study of all children admitted to care over a nine-month period indicated a significant but lower rate of truancy, which may result from differing definitions of non-attendance. Complaints had been received about absence without reasonable excuse by 29% of school-age children. The figure dropped to 25% when only those on compulsory measures were considered. However, among children aged over 12 admitted to care on a compulsory basis, non-attendance was a problem for almost half and nearly three quarters of this group had been reported for difficult behaviour in school (Ramsey 1995).

Research by Francis *et al* (1995) suggests that relying on official complaints or referrals may produce an underestimate of the extent of the problem. Though most of the 27 children in their sample were apparently coping in mainstream schools before coming into care, in fact four had been excluded and social work records indicated that a total of 20 (74%) were experiencing school problems. Again this applied to a higher proportion of secondary than primary age children. The most common problem was aggressive and challenging behaviours.

In their study of teenagers receiving social work services, Triseliotis *et al* (1995) found social work records a poor source of information on school attendance but from these and other sources estimated that non-attendance was a problem before social work intervention for at least 40% of the 116 young people in their study.

These three Scottish studies revealed higher rates of pre-admission non-attendance than reported by Fletcher-Campbell and Hall (1990). In their sample, only 16% of children who had been in care for a minimum of six months had truanted before reception into care. This may reflect the existence of a range of diversion strategies in Scottish authorities, so that children are only coming into care when problems are severe.

Attendance outwith mainstream provision
Kendrick (1995a) and Triseliotis *et al* (1995) reported a high level of alternative educational provision on entering care, either as a result of non-attendance or of behaviour difficulties in mainstream classes. The alternatives included day attendance at residential schools, special day-units, home tutors, intermediate treatment/educational day-care and special college packages. Almost half the teenagers in the latter study were educated outwith mainstream education and 11% were receiving no education at all. Some of these young people were awaiting an alternative placement and others had exhausted all available options.

Children with disabilities
We have been unable to locate specific information about the educational characteristics or experiences of disabled children prior to, or while, being looked after. Indeed there is very little mention of disability within the child-care literature so that this group are in some ways 'invisible'. Given local authorities' duties under the new legislation to promote welfare and to minimise the effects of disability, this represents a significant gap in the knowledge needed to plan services appropriately.

Children who are educationally able
Amidst recognition of the common educational problems amongst children who come into care, it is important to remember that significant numbers are

coping well and will be indistinguishable in educational terms from their peers (Fletcher-Campbell & Hall 1990). Although half of Kendrick's sample had non-attendance problems, half were regular attenders. Similarly, among the teenagers in Triseliotis' study, two girls were taking Highers or A levels, both intending to go to university. Doing well at school and being valued there had helped them, and some others, cope with fraught home situations.

It would be helpful to understand more about the circumstances which have facilitated educational progress among children looked after. Jackson's interviews with 152 young people who had obtained five or more GCSE or 'O' level passes indicated that most felt they had succeeded in spite of, rather than because of, the attitudes of professional staff (Jackson 1994). There is clear evidence, summarised in the following chapter, that admission to care constitutes a serious risk to progress at school for many children.

The role of education in promoting resilience

Education in any setting and at any stage of a care career has a key role in preparing young people for the future, not only in terms of obtaining qualifications but also in equipping them more broadly with life skills. Given that most children looked after will face adverse circumstances in life, the concept of resilience becomes an important element of education.

The idea of resilience has become prominent over the last fifteen years in understanding how some children brought up in adverse circumstances nevertheless appear to do well in later childhood or adulthood. Indeed 'even with the most severe stressors and the most glaring adversities, it is unusual for more than half of children to succumb' (Rutter 1985: 598). The idea of resilience has practical as well as academic value, since it directs attention to factors which enable children to overcome difficult circumstances. The implication is that policy and practice can promote those features of children's lives linked with resilience.

Resilience has been defined as 'qualities which cushion a vulnerable child from the worst effects of adversity in whatever form it takes and which may help a young person to cope, survive and even thrive in the face of great hurt and disadvantage' (Gilligan 1997). In the main, resilience has been studied in longitudinal or retrospective correlational research concerning children who are disadvantaged emotionally and / or materially. The aim has been to identify those factors present during early life that are associated with good later outcomes despite the adverse circumstances.

There are two main reasons why such research is relevant here:

- most children in care face adversity, because they experience a combination of poverty and family instability which leads to them being placed away from home (Bebbington & Miles 1989); prolonged experience of care often brings further discontinuities

- school-related factors have been identified as playing a significant part in resilience.

Resilience is thus a feature of individuals who have good outcomes after bad starts. However, it does not refer only to individual attributes, but also to environmental circumstances. These may be particularly important as there may be more scope for altering a child's physical, social and intellectual milieu, although some personal characteristics are also open to change (for example, self-confidence). A host of factors have been identified as associated with resilience. They may be grouped as follows (Cochran *et al* 1990; Werner & Smith 1992; Fonagy *et al* 1994; Gilligan 1997):

- higher socio-economic status
- relatively fixed individual characteristics, eg above-average intelligence, easy temperament
- more malleable individual characteristics, eg positive coping style, good social skills, self-confidence, sense of efficacy
- positive social and educational experiences, eg presence of a strong supportive and trusting relationship; positive educational experiences.

The most significant in the present context is the last category. This suggests that schooling may be vital in enabling children to make the best of adverse circumstances like being in care, both through offering opportunities for academic success to compensate for the 'failure' in family life and in affording access to alternative supportive relationships – with teachers and with peers. Supportive figures provide important practical help, emotional support, advice and information and role models. Schools also offer opportunities for children to learn coping styles and gain a sense of self worth, thereby enhancing qualities in the third category. Similarly, alternative care arrangements, and in particular the approach of carers, may be crucial in encouraging and supporting children to develop the skills and orientation to life which means they are able to function well in school despite the effects of separation and poverty.

    As much of the research is based on quantification of variables, it often does not indicate very precisely what the key processes which may be involved are. However, it seems clear that positive experiences at school can minimise the effects of adversity and these may be academic, sporting or social in nature (Sylva 1994; Romans *et al* 1995). Experiences of success at school (in whatever domain) can enhance feelings of self-confidence and efficacy, and reduce the chances of alienation from adults and formal institutions. Furthermore, being given responsibilities to assist younger children has been identified as a significant factor in good outcomes for children in adversity (Rutter 1985). For those at risk of educational failure, there is evidence that learning support within mainstream schools may lead to better outcomes than separate arrangements (Maughan 1988). Encouragement, optimism and high, though not excessive, expectations from carers contribute to success in these areas (Borge 1996; Cleaver 1996). Facilitating the development of career-mindedness seems important (Pilling 1992). Teachers and others can help children develop a belief that they are not trapped by their personal history and can be different from other family members they perceive as having failed (Herrenkohl *et al* 1994). A small Canadian study indicated the help gained by young people in care from belonging to school clubs and associations (Silva-Wayne 1995).

Teachers and schools can also help children acquire constructive coping skills. Quinton & Rutter (1988) described 'chain effects' in which school experiences played an important part. They studied young women brought up in long-term residential care (now very rare since younger children are normally placed in foster care). Their data indicated that children who were more reflective and who planned significant life choices concerning partners and work were more successful as individuals and parents when they became adults. This was closely linked to school accomplishments, though usually other than exam success, eg being good at drama, sport or craftwork. Other work has also highlighted the importance for children of developing cognitive skills which enable them to make sense of difficult circumstances and adapt in a considered rather than impulsive manner (Rutter 1988; Fonagy *et al* 1994). An important component can be self-understanding which comprises realistic appraisal of the past and a belief in positive action for the future (Beardslee 1989). The capacity to see difficulties as challenges rather than as overwhelming problems is also important (Antonovsky 1987).

Little is known about how school peer-relationships affect resilience. However, piecemeal evidence indicates that openness and sharing problems related to parental separation or other family instability with school-mates alleviates anxieties and helps children to cope (Mitchell 1985; Frones 1994).

Of course, a mirror image of resilience occurs when children succumb to negative life circumstances, whether because they are particularly susceptible or because they face an accumulation of undermining experiences. Children who are repeatedly abused or who lack continuity of affection tend to acquire internal working models of relationships which make them especially suspicious of relationship commitments and hence resistant to measures aimed at redressing early difficulties (Rutter & Rutter 1993; Fonagy *et al* 1994). Such children are particularly hard for both carers and educational staff to engage.

Consistent findings indicate the qualities of schools which have the best outcomes overall (allowing for factors relating to socio-economic intake) eg purposeful leadership, staff cohesion, family involvement, pleasant work-oriented environments and opportunities for pupils to take responsibility. However it is not known if these qualities work for the small minority of disenchanted young people some of whom will become 'looked after'

(Maughan 1988). It is clear, though, that continuity is a vital aid to developing a sense of self-efficacy and cohesion (Antonovsky 1985), so that unexpected or frequent changes of school tend to undermine resilience.

Summary

School is an important element in the lives of children who became looked after, providing substantial support and care and a forum where children can develop skills and abilities to cope with adversity. There is evidence that teachers' responses to emerging difficulties have a bearing on how effectively children can be sustained at home or be supported on return from a period in care.

The existence of school problems can lead to some children being placed in residential schools, though their primary difficulties may be family-based. There is some evidence that this applies to children with disabilities, though we know very little about the educational needs of disabled children who become looked after.

While many children have school problems prior to becoming looked after, some are indistinguishable from other pupils. Effective encouragement to able pupils is thus as important as support to the most troublesome. As yet, we know relatively little about the factors which may mitigate against a negative care/education spiral.

Positive socio-educational experiences can be a key element in promoting resilience, thus reducing the negative effects of adverse life events. Children's sense of self-worth can be improved through academic progress and developing supportive relationships with teachers and peers. In addition, school offers opportunities to learn effective coping styles and approaches which help in managing difficult situations. School is thus an essential element in equipping children to survive the turbulence of being 'looked after' away from home.

5

Educational Attainment

Evidence that looked after children underachieve in education has emerged from various quarters over the last twenty years, national cohort studies and research on care-leavers being key sources. In addition, the joint inspection by Ofsted and SSI (Ofsted / SSI 1995) demonstrated that educational outcomes for children in care were poor and found little to suggest that much had changed since the Short report in 1984. According to this report:

> Children in care, and particular those who remain in care over a long period, are put at a further disadvantage in respect of their general educational progress and achievement, compared to other children of a similar age and background. It would appear that few children in care attain educational qualifications and that fewer still go on to further and higher education. (Social Services Committee 1984)

This chapter presents key findings on this issue, drawing on the research and inspection-based sources outlined above. Local authorities themselves are able to add very little to this enquiry. With a few notable exceptions (Humberside 1995) local authorities do not routinely monitor the educational progress or attainment of children in their care. It has been suggested that this failure may be both a symptom and a contributing factor to the problem (Fletcher-Campbell 1997; Fletcher 1998).

There are hopes that the introduction of the *Looking After Children* materials (see chapter seven) and closer collaboration between education and social work (see chapter eight) may lead to more detailed information being collated about young people's needs and attainment. This would assist future planning and highlight the most significant gaps in each authority's provision.

Here we review the available information alongside some of the factors which may explain why children in care achieve so little. The consequences for young people when they leave care are also considered.

Evidence from national cohort studies

Drawing on information from the National Child Development Study, Essen *et al* (1976) were among the first researchers to provide evidence of the educational underachievement of children who were, or had been, in care. At age eleven, this group of children were performing below average and those who had come into care before age seven performed worst of all. The average test scores were as follows:

NCDS Average test scores at age 11

	Reading	Maths
In care before age seven	9.2	9.5
In care after age seven	10.1	10.3
Never in care	11.1	11.1

This study also showed that most of the children in care came from very disadvantaged backgrounds, so that social disadvantage itself would have contributed to the poor performance of the 'care' group. However, even after social factors known to correlate with educational failure were allowed for in the analysis, children who had experiences of public care still performed poorly. Compared with children who had never been in care but had similar socio-economic circumstances, children who first came into care before the age of seven scored 14 months below the norm in reading and twelve months below in mathematics. However the authors were reluctant to conclude that the care experience itself 'caused' these low attainments, as both admission to care and poor performance at school might result from severe family problems.

Subsequent NCDS analysis demonstrated a link between behaviour problems at school and being in care. At whatever age they were separated from their families, the behaviour of children in care deteriorated between the ages of seven and eleven (Lambert *et al* 1977).

The Child Health and Education Study (Osborn & St Clair 1987) also set out to examine whether the poor school performance of children in care could be attributed to factors in the child's background rather than the care experience itself. This research involved comparing the attainment of several groups of children who had experienced separation at different ages and for different reasons. These included:

– children who had spent time in care before they were aged five
– children who had experienced a separation from their mothers before they were aged five but had not been in care
– children who had been taken into care between ages five and ten
– children who had been adopted.

The performance of all groups was compared with the national average. The authors confirmed the poor performance of children in care and concluded that this was mainly attributable to their socially deprived backgrounds. Pre-existing behaviour problems which may have contributed to them being received into care were also thought to depress school attainment.

However the children who had been adopted scored above average on behavioural and cognitive measures, despite coming from equally disadvantaged backgrounds as the in-care group. The authors concluded that the advantages conferred by living in child-centred adoptive families had compensated for their earlier deprivation. This fits with other positive findings about adoption outcomes (for example Tizard 1977). An exception to this pattern was identified in recent research by Gibbons *et al* (1995), who found teacher ratings of anti-social behaviour were higher for adopted than foster children (numbers in the study were small, however).

Attainment in foster care

A major study of the educational attainment of fostered children in England has shed further light on how early deprivation and experience in care combine to impact on children's educational attainment (Aldgate *et al* 1993; for a summary see page 121).

The sample consisted of 49 foster children (26 boys, 23 girls) aged 8 to 14. All were in mainstream state schools in one English county and had been in care for a minimum of six months. Many had been in their placements for several years, the mean and median length being six years. Thus, this was a sample of children in fairly stable circumstances, living in what is generally regarded as the optimum form of substitute care available. The foster carers were mostly judged to be interested in helping the children's school work.

Using several standard instruments, children's attainment and behaviour were measured at the start of the study and at yearly intervals over the following two years. Their scores were compared with a control group of 58 children living in circumstances similar to those in the foster children's birth family. Each child's individual progress was measured over a two-year period. The findings were considered to be disappointing. Children in foster care and the comparison group were performing well below the national average but there was no statistically significant difference between the two groups. Thus, despite being in favourable placements, there was little evidence of foster children 'catching up' while they were in care.

Children in foster homes where at least one carer was educated to 'A' level did better on the reading and vocabulary tests. Children placed with these highly qualified carers seemed to have made progress during the early part of the placement before the study began, but did not make further progress during the course of the research. This suggested that early educational intervention may be necessary to secure an 'escape from disadvantage'.

On all three tests and in all rounds of testing, the children who came into care for suspected child abuse or neglect scored significantly lower than did the other foster children. Although there was some evidence of progress in reading, the educational disadvantage of early abuse and neglect was not overcome, even when children were in long-term settled placements.

Information on the children's behaviour indicated a high overall level of behavioural problems amongst foster children but even when there was no evidence of behaviour or emotional problems, foster children scored below the national average in reading, vocabulary and maths. This was not so for children in the comparison group among whom children with no behavioural or emotional problems reached national average levels of attainment.

This research confirms an earlier conclusion from the United States that foster care alone cannot compensate for educational disadvantage (Fanshel & Shinn 1978). In the English study, additional help with reading did lead to improved scores, indicating that special educational inputs are also needed.

The OFSTED/ SSI inspection

This inspection, carried out in four English local authorities early in 1994, indicated that underachievement was more severe among secondary than primary pupils. Only a third of the 60 secondary-age children achieved satisfactory standards in terms of their age and ability and none were judged by their teachers as likely to achieve five subjects at Grade A–C in the GCSE exams, though in 1993 this was achieved by 38.3% of their peers. At primary-school level, of nine children studied closely, five were achieving in line with national norms and others were making progress but their standard of achievement was not in line with either their age or ability. Poor attendance and difficult behaviour contributed to poor performance. Several young people were in crisis or under the threat of care placements breaking down and this uncertainty inhibited progress (Ofsted/ SSI 1995).

Humberside study

A study carried out in Humberside (Humberside County Council 1995) reported that, whereas across the county 95% of children were entered for GCSEs, this applied to less than half the children in care. Of those who were entered for the exam, only 3% achieved 5 passes at A–C grade. This accords with the OFSTED/SSI findings. Young people who had been in long-term care generally fared better than those who were admitted in their teens. More than a quarter of those who were admitted to care at age 10 or younger had obtained at least one A–C pass compared with 11% of teenage entrants. However when those obtaining five passes at A–C were examined, there was no difference in the low proportions of both early and late entrants to the care system. The former group were mainly in stable long-term foster placements, yet fared no better than the more recent entrants who usually had a more chequered care career. This supports Aldgate and colleagues' findings that stable family care does not by itself usually offset earlier educational disadvantage (Aldgate *et al* 1993).

Some young people had obtained other qualifications such as RSA or had made notable achievements in sport, music, drama or community projects. Nevertheless, just under half the children who had been looked after left care with no qualifications whereas the equivalent estimated average for the county, excluding special schools, was 7%.

Leaving-care studies

Given the generally low attainments of most children in care, it is to be expected that they will have poor prospects in making the transition to adulthood (Borland & Hill 1996). A sequence of leaving-care studies undertaken at the University of Leeds have provided ample evidence of care-leavers' poor attainment and the often negative impact of this on their adult lives (Stein & Carey 1986; Stein 1990; Biehal *et al* 1992).

All leaving-care studies have shown that the majority of young people who leave care have no formal qualifications. Stein and Carey (1986) reported that of the young people who took part in their first study in the early 1980s, 90% had no qualifications. The same was true for three quarters of care-leavers surveyed by Garnett (1992) and for two thirds of the 183 young people who participated in a further study in the early 1990s (Biehal *et al* 1992). Only 15% of this group had a GCSE A–C grade or its equivalent and only one young person had an 'A' level. The authors reported that more young people who had been in foster care had obtained qualifications compared with those from residential care. On average, young women did better than men.

As Stein (1994) highlighted, this compares very unfavourably with the position of most young people in this country as assessed in the Economic and Social Research Council's '16–19' study of 5000 young people. They reported that 18% of young people had poor GCSE or equivalent qualifications (Banks *et al* 1992), compared with an average 70% of the care-leavers in the Leeds-based studies who had no qualifications at all.

Not surprisingly, young people's poor educational attainment was reflected in the work they were able to obtain. In their first months after leaving care, the work experience of most young people consisted of temporary work on training schemes, frequent changes and unemployment. Biehal and colleagues (1992) report that within a few months of moving to independence or being legally discharged from care, only 13% were in full employment and over one-third were unemployed Biehal *et al* (1992). Triseliotis *et al* (1995) found most care-leavers were unemployed and living in poverty, too.

As full-time work has becomes generally more difficult to obtain, larger numbers of 16–19 year olds, including care-leavers, are entering further education and training schemes rather than employment. Broad (1997) reports that, despite local authorities' duty under the Children Act (1989) to meet expenses associated with care-leavers' education, few resources are made available. This leads to hardship and presents additional obstacles to young people's success in further education.

Further analysis of the National Child Development Study data also revealed a pattern of few qualifications and high levels of unemployment or low pay amongst former care-leavers. Pilling (1990) followed up the most severely disadvantaged sector, whether they had been in care or not, and confirmed the link between educational achievement and well-being. By age 27, those who had obtained five GCSE O-level passes or equivalent were more likely to be employed, to earn good wages, own their homes, have strong leisure interests and feel satisfied with their lives. This supports similar finding by Banks *et al* (1992). Jackson (1994) also found that over 90% of care-leavers who had five or more GCSEs or equivalent at grade A–C had gone on to some form of further education after school and a higher than usual proportion were in employment.

Cheung and Heath (1994) explored the educational qualifications and occupations of people who had experienced care as children, drawing on data from the 1981 and 1991 sweeps of the National Child Development Study. Overall, they confirmed the familiar pattern of low educational attainment among people who have been in care: 43% had no qualifications compared with 16% among people who had never been in care. In terms of employment, at both 1991 and 1981 the in-care group were more likely to be unemployed or in semi-skilled or unskilled work.

In order to be more precise about the impact of care on future employment over time, the authors distinguished between five categories of care experience and three potential outcomes or scenarios. The five categories of care experience comprised children who:

- entered and left care before age one
- entered and left care before age seven (other than those above)
- entered and left care at or before age eleven (other than those above)
- entered at or before eleven but left after eleven
- entered and left after eleven.

Outcomes were classified as 'optimistic', 'pessimistic' or 'neutral'. In the optimistic scenario, children who have been in care will do better than expected, given their qualifications, as the factors which held back their education gradually lose their force. The optimistic scenario applied for most children in the first group, ie who had entered and left care before age one. Thus short-term care early in life was not associated with educational or occupational disadvantage.

At the other end of the spectrum, the pessimistic scenario means that disadvantaged early circumstances leave a lasting legacy and continue to hamper children's later careers. This applied to the children in the group who had entered care before but left after age 11, a worrying finding which shows care does little to compensate for early disadvantage.

In between is the neutral scenario, meaning children have lower educational attainments than their peers, and their subsequent occupational careers simply reflect their lack of educational qualifications. In other words, the minority of children in care who obtain higher educational qualifications may go on to have the same occupational success as other highly educated children; the majority who obtain low or no qualifications may have the same occupational outcomes as similarly unqualified contemporaries. This neutral outcome applied to the three remaining subgroups. They were educationally disadvantaged but, in occupational terms, they did as well as would be expected, given their qualifications.

Summary

Most children in care are below average in their academic attainments. While there is evidence that early disadvantage and behaviour difficulties are important factors in accounting for the generally low achievement, children's experience of care, and of education whilst in care, appears to compensate for earlier deficits only rarely. Thus part of the problem of poor attainment can be attributed to some aspects of the interactions between the care and education systems.

6

Educational Experience While Away from Home

This chapter focuses on school life. As noted already, this experience is very varied. Though only a few studies or inspections have focused specifically on the topic, relevant information is to be found across a range of subject areas. This chapter draws on a number of information sources, including the views of young people, research, inspection reports, locally-based surveys and guidance on practice in schools.

We begin by outlining relevant aspects of educational policy and guidance on good practice then consider patterns of placement, attendance and school careers. Young people's views about school and research findings about school experience are then presented and the role of specialist provision assessed. In the final section, we turn to the concept of resilience and reflect on ways schools can enhance children's life prospects despite adverse personal, family or material circumstances.

Policy and guidance on good practice

In Scotland, a range of documents provide guidance and discussion of good practice. Circular 4/96 addresses the assessment and recording of children and young persons with special educational needs (Scottish Office 1996c). *Schooling with Care?* is the product of a Scottish Office funded project to identify and disseminate examples of good practice for assisting children and young people who have social, emotional and behavioural difficulties (Munn 1994). This was a collaborative project between social work and education. While its focus was not specifically on young people who are looked after, the issues discussed are highly relevant. The report is accompanied by a video in which young people who have been in care describe their school experiences, then teachers comment on the implications for practice (SOEID/QEC 1994).

Whole-school approaches

A key theme of Munn's report is that effective teaching for children with emotional, behavioural and social difficulties will only occur within a school culture which embraces child-centred principles and values all children as members of the school community. McLean (in Munn 1994) also argues that schools can have a major influence on children's emotional adjustment and behaviour and that staff development has a potentially key role in enabling teachers to develop the necessary skills to manage pupils' behaviour and respond to their emotional needs.

Frier (in Munn 1994) identified six key principles which should underpin practice with children with emotional and behavioural difficulties:

- *Entitlement:*
  Children are entitled to an appropriate curriculum which meets their individual needs within a common framework.
- *Flexibility:*
  Flexible responses, effective teamwork and collaborative approaches are essential.
- *Personal and Social Development:*
  A key educational aim should be to enhance children's self-esteem and social skills.
- *Resources:*
  Imaginative and integrated use of resources is very important. The skill of the class teacher is central.
- *Parents:*
  Valuing home/school contact has to be more than just rhetoric.
- *Pupil Empowerment:*
  Pupils should be involved in planning their own learning and should be able to answer these questions about the curriculum:
  - is it relevant to me?
  - is it worth learning?
  - is it useful to me?

Adopting these principles would provide a sound basis from which to approach the education of young people in care, though, in addition, systems and practices must ensure that the needs of pupils who do not present major problems are also recognised and catered for.

Recommended systems and practices

The Skinner report (Scottish Office 1992) recommended that departments of education and social work should review their arrangements for overseeing the educational needs of children in care, including those excluded from school. It was also suggested that a senior member from education and social work staff should be designated responsibility to oversee the education of children in care.

In England and Wales, the Department for Education and the Department of Health have issued a joint circular on *The Education of Children being Looked After by Local Authorities.* (DfE *and* DOH 1994). This is aimed at teachers and social service staff who have day to day responsibility for the education and care of the children. In addition the Who Cares Trust has produced a guide for school governors (Who Cares? 1996), while The National Children's Bureau and First Key have produced similar guides for teachers (Sandiford 1996; McParlin 1996). Most of these guides aim to help teachers manage the difficult task of paying attention to special needs and making allowances for the upheaval in children's lives, while not labelling them as different or expecting too little of them. Some children find it helpful when teachers and social workers discuss their progress, but others are keen to keep their life at school quite separate. Thus, whatever principles of good practice are introduced, these have to be interpreted in accordance with a child's or young person's individual preferences and circumstances (Fletcher 1998).

The joint circular recommended that head teachers in primary schools and year tutors in secondary schools should hold a watching brief for all children being looked after in their school or year and, where necessary, co-ordinate the pastoral needs of the children concerned. Joint working with social services is viewed as the basis of good practice. It recommends that education staff should contribute to care planning and a copy of a child's care plan should be held in the school file (DfE *and* DOH 1994). Teachers are encouraged to provide robust and individual support but not to be intrusive; to appreciate the stress pupils may be coping with but to have appropriate expectations and encourage them in their education. It is suggested that pupils should be treated the same as others within class, but that time can be made outwith class for discussing difficulties on an individual basis. Teachers are also to encourage carers to give education a high priority.

In his good practice guide for teachers, Sandiford (1996) provides more detail of the knowledge teachers may need or tasks they should undertake to fulfil their responsibilities. He encourages teachers to be aware of pupils' survival strategies and to respond to challenging and testing behaviour, bearing in mind that it may reflect the following:

– sense of loss
– lack of trust in adults
– feeling of rejection
– feeling of isolation
– feeling of confusion
– feeling of being stigmatised
– lack of personal advocacy
– fear of bullying
– feelings of being left behind.

The views of young people have been incorporated in much of the guidance and there is almost complete consensus in the literature about what constitutes good practice. However, in order to benefit from changes in practice, children have to be in school. We now outline patterns of placement and attendance before going on to assess the extent to which children's experience in school reflects the principles upon which policy and guidance are based.

Educational arrangements

As national statistics on arrangements for the education of looked after children in Scotland are not available, relevant information has to be garnered from a range of sources. A survey carried out in Strathclyde provides a useful snapshot (Lockhart *et al* 1996). The survey was undertaken on two days in January 1996 and revealed the following pattern for young people living in children's homes (in other words, not including those in foster care or residential schools):

registered in mainstream schools	60%
registered with training organisations	8%
in alternative education programmes	6%
in employment or further education	6%
not registered	20%

Of those who were registered, more than three quarters were attending on the day of the survey, so over one in five registered pupils were not at school, adding to the similar proportion of non-registered young people.

A national survey which informed the Skinner report, was undertaken in September 1991. It indicated that 46% of young people in residential care in Scotland were in homes which provided education on site (Harvey 1992). This included residential schools.

The Ofsted and SSI report (Ofsted/ SSI 1995) outlined the pattern of educational placement in the four English authorities which were inspected. These were Bradford, Lincolnshire and the London boroughs of Newham and Merton. Unlike the Scottish surveys, this included children in foster care and residential schools as well as those in residential units. The inspection found that three quarters of children were placed in mainstream schooling and an average of approximately 4% were not registered. Special school education was being provided for 10% of pupils and almost 5% were in residential schools or homes which provided education. The remainder were in other provision, including pupil referral units, nurseries and colleges or were receiving home tuition.

Barnardo's carried out a survey of the educational position of children in care in the South and East Belfast Trust (in Northern Ireland care arrangements are part of Health Service provision). A third of the children were perceived as experiencing difficulties at school and around 17.6% had been statemented.

Two thirds of the statemented children were being educated outwith mainstream schools (Sachdev & Taylor 1996).

Based on a study of children in Glasgow children's homes, Tulips (1988) reported that 32% of children were in some form of specialist provision, almost three quarters because of behaviour and emotional difficulties.

Direct comparison across these surveys is not helpful since they each targeted a different group and asked different questions. However they all illustrate that while most children in care remain in mainstream schools, a substantial minority are in varied forms of alternative or specialist provision.

Patterns of school and care careers

Information based on a snap-shot of attendance and/or registration at a particular time is helpful but does not convey any idea of the quality of the schooling experience nor of the pattern of children's education careers over time. Fletcher-Campbell and Hall (1990) provide this kind of perspective. Based on questionnaires completed by social workers on 400 school children in the care of three different English authorities, these researchers identified six groups of children on the basis of their education/care careers as follows:

1. *'No Problems'*: This was the largest category and referred to children with no identified problems or changes of school apart from transfer because of age. There were proportionately more girls than boys in this group, more of them were in foster care and they had been in care and in their present placement for longer then the other groups. Most of them were in mainstream schools and 80% were expected to take GCSE or a higher qualification.

2. *'Only changes'*: These children had no specific problems but had changed school for reasons other than routine transfer. They had been in care for a shorter time than group 1 and were younger. Most were attending mainstream and were thought to be doing well at school.

3. *'Other Problems'*: This group were considered to have other significant problems in school, though they attended regularly and did not have a statement. Half were reported to have behaviour problems, with relationship problems and learning difficulties also reported. This group had the lowest average age and the highest proportion of boys. Most were living in foster care and a high proportion had come into care because of neglect. Most were in mainstream but half were thought not to be fulfilling their potential.

4. *'Stable Statements'*: These children were subject to a statement but had no other problems at school. Compared with the other groups, more were in residential care, they had been in care longer than other groups except group 1 and had had fewer placement changes. In terms of fulfilling their potential, this group came after groups 1 and 2, though social workers' expectations were lower.

5. *'Mere Truants'*: Here truancy was an issue but no other problems were reported. The children were older than the other groups, had come into care more recently and had more links with their family. Nearly a third were living with relatives. All were in mainstream schools and just under three quarters were expected to take GCSE exams. A third were thought to be achieving their potential, though over two thirds were thought to be of average intelligence or above. Despite only being in care for a relatively short time, this group were significantly underachieving.

6. *'Multiple Problems'*: This was the second largest group. They had a combination of problems, including truancy, special needs and suspension. This group had the highest proportion of adolescents and three quarters were boys. They had come into care more recently, two thirds within the last four years and were mostly in residential care. They had a history of disrupted care and education placements and only a third were thought to be fulfilling their potential. Half were considered to be of average intelligence or above and the same proportion were expected to take GCSEs.

The approximate proportions of children in each category were as follows:

no problems	34%
only changes	10%
other problems	11%
stable statements	13%
mere truants	11%
multiple problems	21%

The authors recognised that this classification can only be tentative, partly because social workers have been found to make unrealistic assessments of children's ability, so that their predictions of attainment may be over optimistic (Fletcher-Campbell & Hall 1990; Aldgate *et al* 1993). However the classification is important in that it attempts to link education and care experience and to recognise their impact on each other. More detailed understanding of these links is needed if appropriate needs are to be identified at an early stage.

Levels of exclusion and non-attendance

Concern has been expressed about the general rise in the numbers of children excluded from school, which some attribute to increased competitiveness (see chapter two). For some time it has been recognised that a particularly high percentage of looked after children do not attend school, including a significant subset of excluded children.

The Ofsted/SSI inspectors drew attention to the group of children who did not attend school regularly, some having been excluded or having no educational placement. Overall, 12% of the children were in this category; among 14 to 16 year olds the proportion was 25%.

Comparing children's residential care experience in 1985 and 1995, Berridge and Brodie (1998) reported than non-attendance at school had become a much greater problem. The rate of exclusions was high, even from schools for children with behavioural and emotional difficulties, though school refusal was also a factor.

Several sources indicate that, on any one day, a substantial proportion of looked after children will not be in school. Based on a one-day census, the Audit Commission (1994) reported that 40% of looked after children were not in school for reasons other than sickness. Another single day snap-shot by Maginnis (1993), revealed that 16 (14%) of the 115 school-age residents in the care of Lothian Region were permanently excluded from school, and nine more children were receiving no education whilst an alternative school placement was sought. Children in residential care represented approximately 0.3% of the total secondary school population in the Region, but accounted for nearly one quarter (23%) of the annual total of permanently excluded pupils. Maginnis calculated that the likelihood of a looked after child being excluded was 80 times the average.

The Strathclyde survey showed that one in five children's home residents were not registered at any school, employment or college and almost 40% were absent from school on the day of the survey. Among children of school age, 16% were not registered at school (Lockhart et al 1996). These researchers also provided a breakdown of reasons for non-attendance/ non-registration among the 238 young people involved :

no arrangement for education	36.1%
suspended	7.6%
excluded	5.9%
refusing to attend	6.3%
awaiting placement	7.1%
missing from unit	2.1%
other not authorised	10.9%
illness	8.0%
other authorised	16.0%

There were no arrangements for the education of almost half the girls and approaching a third of the boys who were not at school or college. In addition, there were clear differences across districts in terms of level and reasons for absence. This pattern is consistent with the findings by Brodie and Berridge (1996) that exclusion accounts for a relatively small percentage of non-attendance among children in care.

North Lanarkshire provided information from a survey undertaken on 30 January 1997, indicating that, across their five homes, almost 35% of children of school age were not attending school. Again the reasons included waiting for a school to be identified, exclusion and school refusal.

Francis *et al* (1996) reported the attendance patterns of the 27 young people in their Lothian sample. While all but one of the primary pupils were attending, several of the secondary pupils were not. Tulips (1988) reported that, even among children in specialist provision, non-attendance was twice as high for children in care as for non-care children, with rates between different homes varying widely. He also pointed out that exclusion was fairly common within specialist as well as mainstream provision.

The level of non-attendance clearly continues to be high, even in former regions such as Lothian and Strathclyde where departments of education and social work have operated within a joint policy framework for the last decade. However, exclusion and school refusal accounted for only part of the non-attendance. A significant number were awaiting an appropriate placement.

Explanations of exclusion and non-attendance

The possible reasons for poor attendance at school are many, relating to school or care environment, the young person and the inter-relationship between all three. As noted in chapter four, a substantial proportion of children who become looked after have experienced difficulties which make school an uncomfortable place. In this context the impact of bullying should not be overlooked. We know from children's accounts that being admitted to care can result in persistent teasing, name calling and questioning about their 'problems'. In some instances abuse is also physical. Not surprisingly, research among school pupils has revealed that one way of avoiding bullying is to stay away from school (Rigby 1996; Smith & Sharp 1994). Another response may be to bully others, a course of action which also runs the risk of exclusion.

Fletcher (1995) suggested that 'exclusion' is a general feature of the lives of children looked after. According to her, they are a stigmatised group who feel 'dumped and punished by a care system which also punishes them'. At school they also feel stigmatised by intrusive interest by teachers and social workers, the prejudice of friends or their parents and the genuine concentration problems which come with emotional turmoil. Thus the notion of 'exclusion' extends beyond the formal sanction. Fletcher warns against making exclusion procedures and the associated appeals machinery a 'specialism', and argues that schools should develop broad-based 'inclusion' policies to ensure that these children are given the same educational opportunities as other pupils.

In a similar vein, Blyth and Milner (1994) discuss exclusion as part of a process of societal marginalisation. They link exclusion from school to a wider phenomenon which they term 'civic exclusion' and argue that this process adds to children's disadvantage, leading to high unemployment upon leaving school. Jackson (1995) makes a similar point. Arguing from an English perspective, Blyth and Milner claim that the introduction of league tables and local management of schools have increased the likelihood that troublesome pupils will be excluded from, rather than be supported in, school (Blyth & Milner 1993; 1994).

Research by Brodie and Berridge (1996) also found that head teachers in England were conscious of the pressure resulting from limited resources and an inflexible curriculum when dealing with pupils with educational difficulties. However they challenge the commonly held perception that looked after children are more likely to be excluded because of prejudice towards them (Carlen *et al* 1992), reporting that the number of children living in children's homes who are permanently excluded is usually quite small. Though findings are still tentative, the researchers report that exclusion tends to follow a serious incident preceded by a build-up of tension and is considered justified by the young people, residential staff and teachers. Many of the children had been excluded prior to coming into care, so that looked after status itself had not led to exclusion.

These tentative findings are consistent with a recently completed Scottish study of head teachers' attitudes to exclusion (Cullen *et al* 1997). Children looked after by the local authority did not emerge as a significant category among excluded children and head teachers made every effort to avoid exclusion, which was seen as a failure for the child and the school. Strategies to avoid exclusion included referral to support services within and outwith the school but resources were not always available.

In accordance with one of Cullen *et al*'s recommendations, and drawing on their findings, national guidance on exclusion has recently been issued (Scottish Office 1998d). In the introduction to the guidance, four key elements of the wider policy context which local policy and practice should take into account are identified:

– exclusion from school is seen as a last resort
– the educational needs of excluded pupils must continue to be addressed
– the Government is supporting a series of pilot projects to identify practicable alternatives to exclusion for those pupils at risk
– multi-disciplinary and inter-agency approaches will be necessary to address many of the concerns which give rise to the consideration of exclusion for individual pupils.

The guidance itself clarifies roles and responsibilities in relation to exclusion, within a context of effective whole-school policies. It is suggested that pupils should be consulted in relation to behaviour policies and that their views should be taken into account when schools and local authorities make decisions about exclusion. Monitoring of exclusions is to be more rigorous at school and local authority level. In addition the guidance points out that effective collaboration between education and social work is central to good practice with pupils who are looked after by the local authority.

It is to be hoped that this guidance will contribute to reducing non-attendance among young people in local authority care, the consequences of which are serious and far reaching. Not only do their lives lose structure (Berridge *et al* 1996), they also miss out on the opportunity to obtain qualifications and so reduce the likelihood of 'escaping disadvantage' (Pilling 1990). (We examine non-attendance from the care perspective in chapter seven).

This overview of educational circumstances and attendance highlights that even securing a suitable school placement presents difficulties for a disproportionate number of looked after young people. We now move on to consider their experience when at school, considering first mainstream, then specialist, provision.

Mainstream schools: what young people say

From the leaving-care studies (Stein & Carey 1986; Biehal *et al* 1995), surveys of young people's views (Fletcher 1993) and through young people's organisations, notably Who Cares?, a familiar and consistent picture has emerged of the how becoming looked after affects young people's experience at school. As Fletcher (1993) comments, the answers from the 600 young people who responded to a Who Cares? postal survey provided some stark contrasts: 'deeply disturbing experiences of bullying, stigma, non-attendance and failure and very positive examples of increased motivation and better performance due to the support and security provided by both foster and residential care'.

Many paint a picture of school experience adding to the turmoil of coming into care, rather than being a potential source of stability. Not only do many have to move school, but teachers and peers treat them differently. A key criticism is that these young people are assumed to be academically poor:

> 'Before I went into care I was in top sets and everything. They put me in bottom sets as soon as I moved into care and moved schools.'

> 'I feel that the actual education is no different, but people generally tend to put you in a certain group and because of being in care, people don't expect a lot of you. It's like people in care are classed as 'thick', but there are many who have proved them wrong.'   Fletcher 1993

Young people found that no allowance was made for the upheaval in their lives. Nor were they allowed time to catch up or offered extra help. Coupled with the effects of stereotyping, the consequences could be far reaching:

> 'I mean you get dumped with all the trouble-makers or no hopers because you can't do the work because the teachers won't give you a chance, so you get... what's the word?.... guilty by association. But it's their fault for dumping you with them.'   Biehal *et al* 1995

'Well the school think, as I am in care, I am a trouble maker and I will
not work, but it is not true.'   Fletcher 1993

One change of school is thus, in itself, an educational hazard and children in
care often make many such moves. Not only does changing school entail the
risk of being placed in an inappropriate class, but it may involve delays in
finding a new school. The work may also be somewhat different. Not
surprisingly, young people are critical of the frequent changes and some report
feeling disorientated and unable to focus at school:

'I didn't know what was going on inside my head because I was moving
round so much and I had to start on different pieces of work.'
Biehal *et al* 1995

Some children and young people say that, when people know they are in
care, they treat them differently from other children. Bullying is a common
problem which adds to children's sense of exclusion and low self-worth:

'Ever since I've been in care the kids at school are being nasty to me –
and I get upset because I see them with their family and I'm not.'
Fletcher 1993

Speaking on a video entitled *Teaching with Care,* young people from Who Cares?
Scotland echoed this ever-present feeling of being different:

'You walked about the school thinking "I wonder what they're all
thinking about me" You can't walk around the school with your head
up high.'

As another young woman commented, lack of confidence made you more
susceptible to other people's remarks:

'I didn't have much confidence in myself, just didn't think much of
myself at all, because with other people bringing me down all the time,
I thought, well, that must be the person I am...

Some comments fly out your head but other comments can stick, they
can affect your whole life.'   Teaching with Care 1994

While some of the young people interviewed by Berridge *et al* (1996) were
critical of teachers' uncaring attitudes, they mainly attributed difficulties at
school to the emotional upheaval in their lives. However their comments also
imply that support was not available to help them through:

'Everything went downhill. I didn't care about myself or about school.'

'There was too much going on in my life when I was first in care. I
couldn't concentrate on school work. My life was collapsing and I
couldn't take being bullied and teased at school because of my
problems.'

Much has been written on how to reduce bullying in schools, indicating that the problem has to be tackled at whole school *and* individual level, with action based on clear policy which can be embraced by pupils, staff and parents (Rigby 1996). Strategies to reduce bullying (see for example, SCRE 1993, Mellor 1997) have clear relevance for children being cared for away from home.

What is helpful from teachers?

The young people speaking on the *Teaching with Care* video provided clear indications of what was helpful from teachers, namely to be respected and valued. One young woman differentiated between teachers who 'talked to you as though you weren't really a person and didn't have any feelings' and her register teacher who 'talked to me as though I was somebody.' Another young woman talked of one teacher who conveyed interest and willingness to help, so that she knew she could go and speak to her if she wanted to. A number of young people who took part in the study by Triseliotis *et al* (1995) also had established an important supportive relationship with a teacher.

One request from some young people is that they want teachers to appreciate and make allowances for the impact of living in a residential home, in particular recognising how difficult it can be to have space to do homework:

'I don't always get my homework done due to pressure from home, then I get into trouble at school and it just makes everything worse.'
Fletcher 1993

However others resented teachers' assumptions that less should be expected of them because they were in care:

'Teachers were much more lenient, no work was expected of me. Being at grammar school this kind of treatment was in a way suggesting that I was no longer good enough. Why should the grades change? – after all I'd achieved A grades while being abused.'   Fletcher 1993

These different perceptions highlight that no set formula can be applied to all children. Rather the approach should suit the needs and wishes of each individual. However, most young people are keen that support or special treatment should be offered unobtrusively. Teachers who are oversympathetic, especially in front of class-mates, are felt to be as unhelpful as those who are insensitive. Young people cite two main disadvantages from 'too much care' from teachers: it marks you out as different and it can lead to concentration on your emotional rather than educational needs. The following illustrate the point:

'And the teachers was always asking me if I was all right and making me stand out in a crowd and I didn't like that. That's another reason why I didn't go to school.'   Biehal *et al* 1995

'If people know [I'm in care] I'm teased and called a 'charity scrounger',
also if a teacher knows they treat me different, sympathising, asking
how I am.'   Fletcher 1993

'Sometimes they could be too caring, showing too much sympathy. In
that way you'd still feel you weren't normal, like everyone else… You
still felt different… You're not getting stigmatised in that the teacher's
bearing down on you all the time …it's the opposite 'cos they were
crowding you. They knew there was something wrong and they
wanted to help.'
                                                    Teaching with Care 1994

The same young woman, when asked what she would have wanted from
teachers, answered:

' More support to my class work instead of all the support going into
my emotional needs. There definitely needs to be a balance there – your
educational needs and your emotional needs, it cannot be one or the
other, they've got to come together'.

Naturally, individual young people prefer different levels of interest and
support from teachers but the basic message is that they want teachers to be
available, to treat them with respect and to value their education. Since they
do not want to be treated differently, they want this approach to apply to all
children – or at least for any special attention to be discreet. Thoburn *et al*
(1995) also noted children's acute sensitivity about any special status being
highlighted in class.

Another plea from the young people is that teachers and social workers
should work more closely together. Some young people who have left care
believe that tackling their school problems together might have helped halt
their disruptive behaviour at school and allowed them to have an education.
Many had little sense of school and the home being interlinked (Who Cares?
Scotland, 1998; SOEID/QEC 1994).

However, once again links with schools have to be handled with care.
Intrusive visits by social workers which set them apart from their peers are
not appreciated and many young people are fearful that personal details will
be shared without their knowledge (Fletcher, 1993). A number say they cope
by keeping certain areas of their life private, so it is important that they have
control over what people at school know about them (McParlin 1996).

Positive school experience

For some, coming into care provides an opportunity to concentrate on school
work and have the support of interested carers (Fletcher 1993). Biehal *et al*
(1995) describe the experience of five young women who started to attend

school regularly after coming into care, having previously been kept at home to help parents. For one young woman it was the first time she had experienced stability, praise and encouragement. Though the transition was hard, all these young women had obtained qualifications:

> 'Well it was a bit of a struggle at first, but then it got better…' 'cos I were used to not going to school. But then, you know, I pulled me socks up really and started going full-time.'   Biehal *et al* 1995

> 'School is better because I've worked hard doing my homework. I've done this because I get more encouragement from my carers.'
>   Fletcher 1993

A few of the young people interviewed by Berridge and colleagues (1996) thought that teachers paid more attention to their education because they were in care:

> 'Teachers are more involved because I'm in care. I have more confidence at school. Being in care has helped.'   Berridge *et al* 1996

Similarly, some young people who took part in the study by Triseliotis and colleagues (1995) were pleased that social workers had helped negotiate places in further education which gave them a second chance to obtain qualifications.

Young people who have been in care are particularly vulnerable to certain social and health hazards. Little is known about their exposure and responses to personal and social education, whether in school or from other sources. Most of the teenagers in the Edinburgh/Glasgow study claimed to have had adequate information and advice about sex and HIV/AIDS risks for example (Triseliotis *et al* 1995), but there is a need for such matters to be investigated in more depth.

There is little indication that young people in care have given up on education. Berridge *et al* (1996) asked young people about their attitudes towards education. Of nine young people who were still attending school, four thought school was 'not important ' but the remaining five considered school 'important' or 'very important'. Interestingly, all but one of those who had left school thought it was important and all six had returned to further education to make up for lost opportunities. Help to take up educational opportunities may, therefore, need to extend beyond formal schooling.

In summary, the key issues which young people in care identify as critical to promoting their education are:

- reducing discontinuity through minimising moves and gaps in schooling
- appropriate assessment and expectations of their potential
- supportive school staff who appreciate their vulnerability but focus on their educational needs

- school staff having knowledge of the varying reasons why children come into care and the impact of living in residential care; staff treating this knowledge with confidentiality and sensitivity
- social workers and school staff working together.

Mainstream schools and young people looked after

Perhaps surprisingly, the literature on the education of children in care does not examine their experience within school in great detail. The primary areas covered are young people's attainment and various aspects of the care environment. As reported above, several studies have obtained young people's accounts of school life but there has been no systematic observation of practice in schools. Indeed, as Berridge *et al* (1996) comment, teachers' views have seldom been sought.

This is a significant gap in the knowledge, particularly since differing perspectives are now emerging on some key issues. One of the common criticisms of teachers is that they treat children differently because of their care status (Page & Clark 1977; Fletcher 1993). However, Berridge *et al* (1996) found that all the teachers they interviewed emphasised that children looked after did not present a significantly more problematic group than any other. In fact, teachers said that since the young people in care were such different individuals, it was difficult to perceive them as constituting a discrete group. This awareness of individual difference seems to cast doubt on the suggestion that teachers generally have low expectations of children in care.

The notion that teachers' low expectations contribute to poor attainment was also challenged by the Oxford-based study of children in foster care (Heath, Colton & Aldgate 1994). These researchers found that teachers made realistic assessments of academic ability, whereas social workers were often over optimistic. However these researchers were referring to primary school teachers who presumably have an opportunity to get to know individual children better than do their secondary colleagues.

In the absence of detailed research, the Ofsted and SSI inspection report (Ofsted/ SSI 1995) provides valuable insight into schools' practice in relation to looked after children. The report revealed that children in primary schools fared better than secondary pupils. While all primary school children had access to a broad and balanced curriculum, in some secondary schools modifications to the curriculum had reduced the range of subjects studied for some children. Exclusion, poor attendance and part-time teaching had also limited opportunities to meet curricular requirements. Assessment and recording systems were being developed in most schools but few had an effective system which could map the child's progress quickly. School records were not usually organised in a way which would give a new school a clear picture of the child's educational history and needs. Francis *et al* (1995) also reported that school records on attainment and attendance were incomplete. It was easier to locate information on children who had come into care more recently, possibly indicating improvements in practice but still difficult to get details of attainment in maths and English.

The joint inspection report (Ofsted / SSI 1995) revealed a lack of focused and timely attention to the needs of children in care, especially in secondary schools where responsibility is more diffuse. In primary schools the class teacher had an overview of the child's needs, with a supportive and coordinating role in relation to the child. In secondary schools the identification of a key teacher was less clear. All children had access to normal guidance arrangements but when a child faced a crisis, the personal support was sometimes not sufficiently flexible or immediate to meet the child's needs. The authors pointed out that investing time at crisis points can reduce future stress for the child and school. In terms of accessing support services, children were not always identified early enough. Being looked after did not confer priority for additional action and sometimes the intervention was not flexible or immediate enough to turn around a deteriorating situation. In most schools, there was insufficient guidance on the use of confidential information, only one school having an explicit policy on confidentiality. The children reported that teachers knew too much about their personal lives and head teachers thought that staff allowed knowledge of children's circumstances to influence their expectations.

Based on their review of the schools, care arrangements and collaboration between departments of education and social services, the report concluded that little has been done in practice to boost the achievement of children in care. No strategies were in place to ensure that their education was appropriately planned and monitored, so that individual educational needs continued to be overlooked. In some authorities specialist teaching services for children in care have been developed. Details are included in chapter eight.

Schooling on return home

When children go home from residential or foster placements, this often means a move back to the child's previous school or possibly to yet another new school. Bullock *et al* (1993) examined in some detail the significance of returning to mainstream school at the end of a period of being looked after. They pointed out that the educational issues, though crucially important to the children themselves, were given far less attention by social workers than reintegration into the family. The authors highlighted how stressful children found being the 'new boy' or 'new girl' at the centre of attention. One child was quoted as saying:

> Everyone just asked questions. Because you'd been in a children's home they thought you were a criminal, they asked "What did you do? "How much did you nick?", "Did you try to kill someone?"

Bullock and colleagues note that entry or return to school is easier at the primary than secondary stage and that planned returns are easier to manage than highly mobile children who disappear and reappear in school without notice. Referring to work by Fleeman (1984) and Pickup (1987), they emphasised the potential help of an induction programme which encompasses senior staff working closely with social services, good school/family contact and a particular teacher being available for counselling. At secondary level, school organisation did not always facilitate contact with a particular teacher but pupils themselves showed considerable ability to seek out supportive teachers. The authors suggest that linking with an older pupil can also be helpful and conclude that the importance of having a sympathetic person within the school cannot be overestimated.

In their conversations with teachers, Bullock and colleagues were surprised to find that teachers found it difficult to conceptualise the return to school as an issue. There was often 'little notion of the child having a 'social' career or that problems in one area could compound problems in another'. This approach resulted in one boy being allocated to classes simply on the basis of psychometric testing, with little consideration given to his social networks.

The researchers found that the concerns of children were concrete and immediate. Unfamiliarity with the layout of the building, routines and school equipment caused considerable anxiety, especially since getting it wrong could lead to public ridicule. The authors paint a graphic picture of the newcomer's experience:

> The newcomer, as she enters the school gate is an object of considerable interest, something bright on an otherwise sepia landscape. Everything they do is public, scrutinised by an audience of peers anxious for a laugh at someone else's expense. There is competition and jostling for position besides which scholastic achievement takes second place. Thus, taking off one's clothes for gym, the chilly trip to the swimming bath, grabbing a seat at lunch time, waiting for the bus, all anxiously loom in the child's mind long before the bell rings, like a morning on the Somme, a trill that signifies you are going over the top, alone and without a comforting swig of rum.

Farmer and Parker (1991) found that teenagers with special educational needs were more likely to settle with their families on return home when appropriate education was provided in a specialist setting. Of the 'disaffected' group, (ie mainly teenagers who had been involved in offending), 37% returned to a specialist educational setting.

We now turn to review young people's experiences of and views about specialist educational provision.

Specialist provision

As we noted earlier in this chapter, a substantial proportion of children in care are not educated in mainstream but in specialist units, on a day or residential basis. Many are outwith mainstream school before coming into care (Kendrick 1995a; Triseliotis *et al* 1995), the majority in provision for children with social, emotional and behavioural difficulties.

Types of specialist provision

Alternative provision in Scotland comes in many forms. As outlined in the 1990 HMI report, at one end of the range there are small residential schools with varying approaches which offer a different life experience to pupils:

> Some saw their role as providing disturbed pupils with the optimum conditions for personal growth, by substituting for conflict and alienation, stable patterns of living and opportunities for achievement. A second approach emphasised the creation of a social community in which all staff and pupils participated and continuous evaluation of behaviour by staff, peer group and self. A third gave priority to processes and activities which enabled children to gain insights into themselves and their predicaments.

At the other end of the spectrum were specialist services based in mainstream schools, drawing on guidance and support staff. Some were developing home/school contact and beginning to evaluate and address the factors which might alienate pupils from learning.

In between were a range of provisions including: specialist assessment and treatment centres, larger residential schools (some of which also take day pupils), separate day schools for disturbed or difficult pupils, day units separated in varying degrees from mainstream school, day units within mainstream schools. There were also a few projects which provided social work support and remedial help 'and sometimes simply refuge and relief'.

Staffing in alternative units is also variable Some have a combination of teaching and social work staff. They can be managed by social work, education or a voluntary organisation. A number of writers highlight the danger that teachers in specialist units can become marginalised and out of touch with current developments in the curriculum (Fletcher-Campbell & Hall 1990; SWSI 1996; Berridge & Brodie 1996).

Effectiveness of specialist provision

In their review of the literature on the effectiveness of alternatives to mainstream schooling, Cullen and Lloyd (1997) point out that, given the diversity in provision, effectiveness is an illusive concept. They suggest that the service can be judged against three criteria: general principles; specific aims and purposes of the provision; and individual needs.

One of the key principles is integration. Cullen and Lloyd examine the child's right to integration within the education system and, based on the Salamanca Statement (UNESCO 1994), outline three main strands within British policy:

- the right to be educated in a suitably resourced mainstream environment
- the right to be educated in the least restrictive environment which accords with the safety of self and others
- the right to remain in mainstream school and own home if possible, to stay in own community if possible.

The authors note that, while for children with other special needs their right to integration in mainstream is strongly argued, in relation to children with emotional and behavioural difficulties, the argument usually centres around their right to the least restrictive environment or to the environment which least intrudes upon their family and community network. This group of children have little public support and, without adequate resources, their presence can adversely affect the education of others.

Widely differing views emerge from the literature on the extent to which alternative provision meets the need of children. On the one hand there are concerns that the curriculum is narrow and that insufficient attention is paid to educational attainment (Dunbar 1987; HMI 1990; Ofsted & SSI 1995). In contrast, others argue that the broader-based approach to education is one of the strengths of specialist provision, incorporating recognition of achievements that may remain ignored in mainstream schools (Dean 1992, cited in Cullen & Lloyd 1997). Indeed, many commentators consider that personal relationships between children and staff in residential homes are part of the positive educational experience (Dunbar 1987; Dean 1992; Cooper 1993; Howe 1995, cited in Cullen & Lloyd 1997).

Looked after children in specialist provision

For young people within the care system, attendance at alternative schooling often follows a period during which they have had no education at all. In their studies of children involved in the care system, Kendrick (1995a) and Triseliotis *et al* (1995) found considerable enthusiasm for day and residential units among the pupils and parents alike. When a decision to place children in specialist provision was first made, young people and social workers often began with a sense of failure or trepidation, but most came to value the benefits of the educational and social environment. Interestingly, it was frequently parents who had been pressing for the placement to be made.

A key asset identified by both social workers and young people were the smaller classes, individualised attention and programmes, and the reduced pressure to live up to expectations set for pupils without difficulties. Young people also liked the experience of learning to spell or do maths and being able to make progress in a smaller number of subjects. Staff who understood and accepted them were also appreciated. Half of the young people had a 'key teacher' who would help with any problems and act as co-ordinator. Young people's comments illustrate what they liked:

> 'People don't laugh if you don't know things. You don't feel stupid if you don't understand. Teachers explain, the work is not hard.'

> 'Classes are smaller. Everyone is in the same boat, they all have the same kinds of problems so you don't feel awkward.'

> 'It's not hard work at all. There's only five people in the class. The teachers go over things all the time and help.'

> 'I can spell better'… 'I'm better at maths.'   Triseliotis *et al* 1995

Most parents were also positive, though some complained about the distance young people had to travel and voiced concern about the stigma associated with special schooling. The adverse influence of other pupils worried some (Triseliotis *et al* 1995). Both Triseliotis and Kendrick (1995a) reported that as availability of alternatives was patchy, some young people had to wait a considerable time for a place and / or travel substantial distances every day.

Residential schools

Because it is expensive and involves the removal of the child from the community and mainstream education, residential school is not a preferred option in social work policy and practice. Residential schools have also been accused of neglecting children's emotional and care needs. Grimshaw and Berridge (1994) undertook a study across four schools and were critical of unclear admission procedures, the lack of interdisciplinary work and the absence of consultation with children. Only a third of their sample were looked after by the local authority, the remainder being 'children in need'. The authors make the point that removing children labels them as deviant and as being 'the problem' rather than as 'having problems' which may be located in the family or school. The numbers entered for GCSEs and other qualifications varied widely across the four schools in their study. In Scotland most residential schools now expect to present children for Standard Grade exams.

HM inspectors' reports on some residential schools have indicated that the range of subjects offered is sometimes limited and that more emphasis is needed on progress and attainment across the curriculum (Scottish Office 1997–98). However staff are generally supportive towards pupils, there is good communication with care staff and some schools have established helpful links with parents. Certain grant-aided and independent schools are now subject to the same registration and inspection standards as other residential accommodation for children and there is a duty to promote the welfare of the resident children, whether or not they are looked after by the local authority (Scottish Office, 1997b).

A positive view of residential schooling also emerged from the studies by Kendrick (1995) and Triseliotis *et al* (1995). Focusing primarily on residential schooling provided by voluntary organisations or local authorities within Scotland, they encountered a number of young people who, after months or years of not receiving any education, achieved some educational success within residential schools. In terms of the teaching, young people liked the same features as were outlined in relation to other alternatives, ie small classes, individual attention and the opportunity to learn.

Parents also found residential schooling a valuable source of support:

> 'T. is away but not separated from us. You get a break during the week but she is home at weekends. If we have problems we can phone the school and they take it up with her when she goes back.'

> 'I liked everything about it – small classes and teachers and staff were nice and concerned. He obviously benefited, especially educationally.'   Triseliotis *et al* (1995)

This study and the one by Kendrick (1995a) both reported that most placements in residential schools were long-term, though in Kendrick's study, a few were short-term 'holding' or 'respite'. The stability of staff and residents seemed to be a positive factor, especially compared with residential units.

The residential schools were dealing with children who had significant difficulties. Using the Rutter scale (Rutter *et al* 1970), social workers placed 70% of the residential school pupils in the most difficult category. On the other hand, in most instances their family situations remained intact and many went home at weekends. The most common reasons for admission were primarily offending/behaviour problems or non-attendance at school, though two pupils in Kendrick's study had come into care initially for child protection reasons.

The short-term outcomes for residential school placements were very positive (Hill *et al* 1995; 1996). A number of questions about the outcome of care placements were posed: had aims been met? how satisfied were social workers? had the placement lasted as long as planned and needed? had placements helped with original difficulties? had they benefited the young person? According to social workers, parents and young people, nearly all the residential school placements had succeeded on each criterion. On all measures, residential schools were rated more positively than children's homes. Parents and young people liked the structure and social workers considered that staff in residential schools were more plentiful and more skilled that staff in residential units (Triseliotis *et al* 1995).

Social workers considered that for 88% of the young people in residential schools there had been an increase in self esteem during the year of the study. In contrast, only 40% of those living in residential units were thought to have an enhanced self-image. Some social workers talked of young people having 'blossomed' in quite unexpected ways. The Coopersmith measure of self esteem showed a similar, though less marked, trend (Coopersmith 1990). Young people themselves talked of a sense of achievement in a wide range of activities and of being better able to manage socially. Social workers considered that 90% of residential school placements had improved school performance and three quarters of the young people agreed.

Similarly positive views were expressed in Kendrick's study. Social workers considered almost half the placements had achieved their aims. Over half the placements were rated by social workers as 'good', only two as 'poor'. Seven had not achieved their aims, of which six had broken down. School staff talked of the importance of structure and routine which they contrasted with chaotic life at home or in children's homes. Social workers also acknowledged the positive side of close supervision, high pupil/ staff ratio and fewer opportunities for mischief, aspects also appreciated by young people and their parents (Kendrick 1995a).

The researchers in these studies do not advocate that placement in residential school should necessarily become more common but suggest that the effective characteristics might be replicated in other care and school settings. In both studies some social workers, teachers and parents regretted the placement had come so late. So much education had been lost that the Standard Grade curriculum had to be crammed into six months and, despite progress, no time was left to get back into a mainstream school. The HMI report (HMI 1990) also commented on the negative impact of going through every available option instead of taking radical action at an early stage if a need for specialist measures is indicated.

Neither study was able to follow the young people for long enough to see whether the short-term benefits persisted after leaving school. Evidently residential school is not a positive experience for all young people. Both studies included examples of young people whose disruptive or dangerous behaviour escalated and who moved thereafter into secure accommodation.

Education in secure accommodation

Educational provision was assessed in a Social Work Services Inspectorate report on secure accommodation (1996). Young people reportedly valued the commitment and concern which their teachers showed them and teachers' use of imaginative means to motivate the pupils was praised. Young people themselves paid tribute to teachers who had convinced them of the value of education. Teachers had access to a range of curricular packages which helped them to devise individual programmes within the 5–14 framework. The best approaches involved care staff and teachers working together and it was recognised that much social education could take place outwith the classroom, especially at evenings and weekends.

Criticisms centred on poor arrangements for assessing young people's educational needs and accessing prior records, insufficient attention to the curriculum at management level and lack of clarity on educational policies. There was also concern that learning support had not been developed for a small number of pupils with very low standards in reading, writing and maths. These pupils were thought to need counselling to help them recognise their difficulties and come to believe that they were capable of learning.

The resilience research and theorising suggest that positive cycles may be promoted for children in care. Academic, social or recreational aspects of education in which a child is particularly interested and has potential for success should be identified and encouraged by carers. These can, in turn, make the child more responsive to the care experience, as well as 'banking' academic and psycho-social assets likely to assist in adult life. Success in at least one area can also help avoid a downward spiral of low expectations and mutual antipathy between child and teacher. A sustained, close, supportive relationship with at least one teacher is also likely to pay dividends beyond any immediate learning benefit. The potentially positive contribution of peer support should be recognised, too, rather than presuming that peer influences are inevitably negative.

As yet, the resilience literature has mainly identified what needs to be done, rather than detailing how it may be done. It is also important to remember that the precise qualities which define and develop resilience will vary according to the cultural context (Van Gendt 1994) and the nature of available opportunities (Pilling 1988). However, this approach does support a positive frame of mind and indicate in broad terms some of the requirements for helping children who may otherwise appear to have poor prospects and little hope.

Summary

This chapter has reviewed several aspects of experience in school. It is encouraging that guidance on good practice is now available and that this reflects the views and wishes of young people. The provision of non-stigmatising support through a key teacher is central. The concept of resilience has highlighted the potentially significant role of schools in helping young people develop ways of coping with adversity. For some young people, coming into care provides their first opportunity to concentrate and make progress at school. However, a disproportionate number of children attend school infrequently, whether by choice, through exclusion or because no suitable placement can be found. Young people themselves are often critical of how they are treated at school and prefer teachers who are understanding but who focus on their academic work rather than their emotional problems. Many would like social workers and teachers to work together more effectively but there are also fears about confidentiality. Young people need to be consulted about what personal information should be shared.

Two large Scottish studies have reported positive outcomes for placements in residential schools. Pupils and parents were generally enthusiastic about specialist provision in day or residential units, though some young people started this too late to derive the maximum benefit. HM Inspection reports are adding to understanding of developments within this sector.

7

The Care System and its Impact on Education

Having considered how young people fare within school, this chapter examines aspects of the care system which have a bearing on that experience. As noted in chapter one, relatively little research or writing has focused specifically on how being looked after impacts on children's educational experience. There is however a wider literature about various aspects of the care system and some of this has a direct bearing on this issue. Thus, in common with the preceding one on school life, this chapter's focus is wide. We begin by briefly reviewing policy and practice in relation to children in public care then go on to look at social workers' attitudes and expectations. Discontinuity and lack of an effective parent are often cited as disadvantages of being looked after; we examine the consequences for children's education. Finally the impact of living in residential or foster care is considered.

Developments in child-care policy and practice

Sonia Jackson, who has been highly influential in drawing attention to the education of children in care, partly attributes the neglect of this issue to the tendency of child-care policy and practice to accord a higher priority to emotional well-being than to academic achievement (Jackson 1989). This brief review of developments in social work approaches helps place current practice in perspective.

Jackson points out that, prior to 1948, training was an important part of residential care while the expressive needs of children were largely ignored (Jackson 1989). Increasing awareness of the importance of social relationships and attachment (Bowlby 1951) prompted changes in practice with a preference for family placement. Within residential care, there was increased emphasis on emotional well-being and less on preparation to take up a trade or go into service (Mahood 1995). While these developments were largely positive, Jackson argues that failing to equip children to earn a living does them a disservice.

During the 1970s, concerns were raised about large numbers of children 'drifting' in residential care with little hope of returning to their parents (Rowe & Lambert 1973). At the same time evidence was emerging that older children were able to form attachments to substitute carers, and through this overcome the effects of earlier deprivation or loss (Tizard 1977). The Children Act 1975 facilitated placements with substitute families and several schemes were set up across the country to promote long-term family placement, where possible on the basis of adoption (Thoburn *et al* 1986; Borland *et al* 1991). Establishing attachment to a reliable carer was seen as crucial to promoting the emotional well-being of children separated from their families of origin and all other considerations, including educational progress, were subordinate to this central aim.

While issues of attachment and emotional development remain central to any service concerned with caring for children (Howe 1996), it is now recognised that addressing issues such as education and health simultaneously can promote rather than detract from emotional well-being (Aldgate *et al* 1993; Ward 1995). Gilligan (1997) suggests that in terms of equipping children for life, it may be more useful to concentrate on 'resilience' than 'attachment'. The concept of resilience applies equally appropriately to children who are looked after for short periods as to those who require a substitute family. The role of education in promoting resilience was considered in chapter four.

The local authority's duties under the Children (Scotland) Act 1995 to 'safeguard and promote the welfare' of looked after children, to prepare them for when they are no longer looked after, and to promote contact with members of the natural family, might be viewed as a general requirement to promote resilience. The guidance to the Act (SWSG 1997) emphasises the importance of education alongside other significant aspects of children's lives such as health and social relationships. Good communication between schools and social work, closer monitoring of attainment and a proactive approach to problems are all to be developed through more systematic planning and reviewing.

A system to promote more child-centred and proactive care for children looked after has been developed in England (Parker *et al* 1991; Ward 1995). The *Looking After Children: Good Parenting Good Outcomes* project has devised a system for promoting best practice in caring for children and introducing ideas about outcome into social work practice. Based on research, consultation and piloting in England, this Department of Health funded project has developed a set of materials for recording information, reviewing progress and ensuring children's needs are met while they are looked after. As the title suggests, the system is based on the principle that local authority care should strive to replicate good parenting and aim to achieve good outcomes for young people. Amended for use in Scotland, these materials are being piloted by eleven local authorities during 1997–98 and their implementation evaluated (Wheelaghan *et al* forthcoming).

Included in the *Looking After Children (LAC)* materials is a set of assessment and action records. These six age-related records are used to assess children's progress in relation to the care they receive across seven key dimensions: Health, Education, Identity, Family and Social Relationships, Social Presentation, Emotional and Behavioural Development, Self Care Skills. In addition to assessing needs, the records prompt professionals to identify those actions required to cater for them. The records are designed to encourage communication and collaboration among all those involved in children's care, including birth parents. Children and young people should also be involved in the process as far as possible. The records for older children are, in fact, designed to be completed by the young people themselves, together with a relevant adult.

Legislation, policy and systems to encourage best practice are therefore now in place to promote increased attention to the educational needs of young people within the care system. However experience in England indicates that, on its own, such a framework will not change practice (Ofsted/SSI 1995) Attitudes and expectations of social workers and care staff are also central to the development of a more proactive approach to children's education.

Social workers' attitudes and expectations
Social workers have been criticised for according education a low priority. Here we consider some findings on: the importance social workers attach to education; their expectations of children in care; their knowledge of the education system.

The importance of education
Jackson is very critical of social workers for failing to appreciate the importance of education as a potential route out of disadvantage and a means of enhancing self esteem (Jackson 1989, 1994). These criticisms are echoed by Gilligan who finds it curious that social work, whose defining characteristic is its emphasis on social context and experience, should lose sight of the fact that after the family, school is the most powerful influence on children's development. In an article which aims to change this perspective, he outlines the evidence that school is a vital source of educational and social experiences, pointing out that the benefits are in fact greatest for children living in adverse circumstances (Gilligan 1998).

There is indeed considerable evidence that social workers have not generally placed education at the top of their agenda. Knapp et al (1985) reported that though half the children in their sample were assessed as having school-related difficulties, educational improvement was a specific objective for only six of them. Of 285 objectives listed by social workers, only 16 related to education. Similarly Aldgate et al (1993) found that social workers allocated 'attending to children's educational attainment' and 'helping children develop special talents' a low priority, their primary focus being 'helping children make special attachments'. Francis et al (1995) reported similar findings.

Long-term foster or adoptive parents report that there has often been poor assessment of children's educational difficulties while in public care with the result that by the time the children are placed with them, some problems have become entrenched (Quinton *et al* 1997; Borland *et al* 1998). Ward (1995), reporting on the *Looking After Children* project, found that, if the child was not attending school, some social workers left the section on education blank rather than identifying what action was needed to remedy the situation. Some social workers' comments during the pilot of these materials indicated another source of reluctance to promote educational progress actively. There were objections to the questions in the forms which asked about children's access to libraries, believing that encouraging access to books and parental reading was encouraging middle-class values and unrealistic aspirations amongst deprived children (Ward 1995).

Both Jackson (1989) and Aldgate (1990) suggest that ambivalence about the education of children in care reflects remnants of Poor Law notions of 'less eligibility'. According to this point of view, children in public care should not receive attractive or expensive support to education, since this disadvantages children still living with their families and might act as an incentive to go into care. On the other hand, in the Edinburgh/Glasgow study of teenagers, school matters were reported by both social workers and young people to be one of the main topics discussed when they met (Triseliotis *et al* 1995). Sometimes, though, this was largely a matter of information-sharing rather than active intervention.

Expectations of children in care

From the accounts of children who have grown up in care, we know that many experienced indifference on the part of social workers and carers as far as their education was concerned (Kahan 1979; Triseliotis & Russell 1984; Jackson 1994; Teaching with Care 1995). Referring to her own study of children who had grown up in care and been educationally successful, Jackson (1994) indicated that their success owed little to the support and encouragement of social workers: 'Their most consistent response was that their ability had not been recognised or their achievement recognised by social workers and residential care workers'. Jackson is particularly critical of policies in the 1970s which encouraged adopters and carers not to have too high expectations of children (DoH 1970). More recently, some social workers' responses to the LAC assessment and action records have reflected a similar reluctance to set standards for children, fearing this would compound feelings of failure (Ward 1995).

From their interviews with adults who had been adopted or grown up in residential care, Triseliotis and Russell (1984) concluded that while supportive interest was very much appreciated, too high expectations or ambitions placed children under pressure: 'They wanted me to get on, that I know. I am afraid I just wasn't that type. I was unhappy about their ambition… they were pushing you… all I wanted was to get away and try to be myself'.

The view that social workers expect little of children educationally is challenged by Aldgate *et al* (1993). Compared with foster carers and teachers, social workers were more optimistic about children's future attainment. They thought all children would get some qualifications and expected 63% to gain at least five GCSEs. Just under a fifth were expected to pass 'A' levels and half of these were expected to go on to higher education. These are highly optimistic expectations compared with evidence of how children currently leaving the care system have fared. As noted in chapter five, Biehal *et al* (1995) reported that between half and three quarters of young people leave care with no formal qualifications. The high expectations of the social workers in the study by Aldgate and colleagues may indicate that they were out of touch, rather than that they were actively seeking to promote better attainment. In the Aldgate study, teachers' expectations were much lower, and comparison with standard test results indicated that their less optimistic assessments were accurate. Similarly, teachers' predictions, reported in the Ofsted / SSI report (1995), that none of the children in care would gain five GCSEs at grade A–C may be depressingly realistic. Teachers are in a better position than social workers to assess pupils' educational prospects, though there are clearly risks that low expectations will be self-fulfilling.

Social workers' understanding and knowledge of education

Fletcher-Campbell and Hall (1990) also claimed that social workers were over optimistic and described their views on children's educational performance as 'subjective and unreliable'. They reported that social workers did not accept that children were underachieving and were ill-informed about what their education entailed. They were also critical that discussion at reviews focused on attendance or behaviour rather than academic progress, pointing out that this conveys to the child that the latter is of minimal concern. Jackson (1989) also referred to social workers' poor assessments of children's intellectual ability. She claimed social workers tend to conflate performance and behaviour.

Fletcher-Campbell and Hall argued that while teachers have taken on some of the social work agenda, for example in terms of learning about child protection procedures, few social workers have had in-service training on the national curriculum or other developments in education. The view that social workers are ill-informed on general educational matters and on individual children's performance was borne out by the Ofsted / SSI report. Few social workers knew much about children's abilities, past achievements and educational needs prior to placement. Berridge *et al* (1996) reported that some residential carers were unsure whether or not children were subject to a statement of special educational needs (the equivalent of a record of needs in Scotland). This lack of understanding reinforces the need for teachers to make more detailed input at child-care reviews as advocated by Francis *et al* (1995).

Continuity and discontinuity
Moves of placement and school

Continuity of relationships at home, with teachers and with peers, as well as consistency of lessons and educational programmes, are important foundations for satisfactory achievements. Yet the experience of most children looked after away from home for more than a short period is of discontinuity in all these respects.

One of the main explanations offered for the poor educational attainment of children looked after and living away from home is that moving around disrupts their attendance and learning at school. There is ample evidence that frequent moves are a feature of life in residential and foster care and that moves are not necessarily prompted by the needs of the children. Berridge (1985) reported that in a sample of 234, one third had experienced five or more moves since coming into care. Berridge and Cleaver (1987) indicated that moves in foster care were more often prompted by foster family and/or agency needs (such as the classification of some placements as emergency, short-term or for assessment) rather than child-related factors. The findings of Francis *et al* (1995) suggested that moves in care were more likely for children of secondary school age. Although numbers in the study were small, over a two year period, none of the primary school, but 87% of secondary school children, experienced at least one placement change. Triseliotis *et al* (1995) found that a scarcity of suitable placements led to a series of temporary placements for some teenagers.

Unsurprisingly, in many instances, entry to care or moves of placement also necessitate a change of school. Cliffe and Berridge (1991) examined the impact of Warwickshire's policy to close all its children's homes. They concluded that one drawback was the increased number of moves for some children who experienced multiple fostering breakdowns. Since family placement resources were stretched, there was less scope for choice or matching to take educational issues into account. They reported that almost half the moves (45%) required the children to change school or to undertake a more difficult journey to get there. In only a minority of instances (14%) did the move appear to confer benefits in terms of education.

Among the sample in Kendrick's Scottish study, almost three fifths of the school age children changed school or alternative educational provision during the study year, either at admission or at a later change of placement. (This included young people coming into care because of school problems and moving from mainstream to specialist provision). A third of these changes involved a single move, but one in seven had moved twice and one in 16 had three or more changes in the course of the year. As well as interfering with educational continuity, changing school can cut a child off from sources of support from teachers and peers (McAuley 1996).

Berridge and Cleaver (1987) reported that when children had to move school on joining a foster family, the placement was more likely to break down. In their study of children returning home from care, Farmer and Parker (1991) found that half the 'disaffected' group (mainly older children) had been in three or more placements with corresponding changes of school. They suggest that it is therefore unsurprising that nearly two thirds had attendance problems on returning home. However disruption to education is not inevitable. Fletcher-Campbell and Hall (1990) found a third of children in care had experienced a stable school life and there had been continuity in education of half of the 18 children whose circumstances were examined in detail as part of the Ofsted/SSI inspection.

Francis et al (1995) noted that when there were changes of placement and school, it was not always moves in placement which prompted the educational disruption. On the contrary, of the thirteen instances in which there were changes of both care placement and school, eleven (85%) were prompted entirely or partly by school-related matters. For this group of children, education difficulties were more likely to contribute to change of placement than vice versa. The authors concluded that close liaison between social work and education is needed to anticipate when difficulties are likely to occur.

These findings highlight the complex relationship between care and school careers about which, as Fletcher-Campell and Hall (1990) note, we have very little understanding.

It seems likely that frequent moves will have an impact on school attainment. Biehal et al (1995) found that young people who had experienced a high number of moves in care were most likely to have no educational qualifications. Three quarters of those who made four moves had no qualifications compared with only half who had no moves. However the educationally successful care-leavers in Jackson's study had moved often and still managed to obtain five GCSE passes at grade C or above. The average number of moves was 5.6 for men and 4.6 for women; over a quarter had had between five and ten placements and two reported 30 or more. Among this group, other factors such as strong support from a carer had compensated for lack of continuity (Jackson 1994).

Continuity in education across the care continuum

Avoiding unnecessary moves while in care is evidently important for emotional security as well as educational progress (Parker 1988), so that the availability of a suitable range of placements within travelling distance of children's schools is crucial (McAuley 1996). However the literature indicates that promoting continuity in education extends beyond reducing placement moves and requires close collaboration between social work and education at each stage of a child's care experience. As noted in chapter three, for many children who are looked after away from home, this is a short, though possibly upsetting, episode in their lives. Parker (1980) argued that schools are a potential source of continuity for any child who is required to move around so that attendance at their home school throughout a period of being looked after should be encouraged. On the other hand, Fletcher-Campbell (1990) observed that the desirability of continuity may have to be considered alongside the demands of an excessively long day, if staying at the usual school requires considerable travel. Decisions about the most appropriate option are presumably taken before or shortly after admission to care. At this stage, teachers rarely contribute to planning and close collaboration between social work and educational services is unusual – except in the case of residential schooling (Ofsted / SSI 1995; Francis *et al* 1995).

The Skinner report (1992) recognised the value of continuity in schooling but also recommends that if a child is required to change school, this should be planned in close cooperation with the school, avoiding delay in being assigned to appropriate classes. As noted in chapter six, children also need support to reintegrate into school after a stay away from home (Bullock *et al* 1993).

Corporate parenting and effective links with schools
Parents' contribution to schooling
The Plowden Report (DES 1967) and Warnock Report (DES 1978) recognised the importance of parental involvement in children's educational development, especially in relation to children with special educational needs. Several studies have demonstrated the effectiveness of parental involvement in teaching children to read (Menmuir 1994). The advantages of having middle-class parents have long been recognised (Jackson & Marsden 1966). Parker *et al* (1991) reported that the child's progress in infant school was strongly influenced by the amount of parental contact with and knowledge about the school, independent of social class. Many parents of disabled children make strenuous efforts to get the best services. There is thus clear evidence that children benefit from having parents who are interested, well informed and able to promote their children's best interests within the school.

In this section we consider the extent to which local authorities are acting as effective parents in terms of promoting the educational opportunities of looked after children. It has been recognised for some time that impersonal local authority departments do not make very effective parents (Parker *et al* 1991). In relation to education, the service is found wanting in three key elements: taking a personal interest in the child's educational progress, clarity about roles and maintaining effective contact with the school, and providing the kind of home environment which promotes educational progress.

Personal interest and commitment

Jackson (1987) stated that the lack of personal investment in children in care over a life-time means no-one takes an interest as ordinary parents do. Similarly Parker *et al* (1991) argued that local authorities are seldom as discriminating or proactive on behalf of children they are looking after as parents in ordinary households, for example by checking out thoroughly which schools would be most suitable for their children.

Adopters and long-term foster parents provide evidence of the importance of parental advocacy and of local authorities' failure to replicate this for children in care. Adoptive parents interviewed by Borland *et al* (1998) talked of devoting considerable energy to advising schools of their children's needs, mostly in relation to emotional and behavioural difficulties. This included regular discussion and providing appropriate literature and advice for teachers on how best to respond to particular behaviour. They also maintained very close links and advised the school on changes which might upset the child.

Quinton *et al* (1996) describe similarly intensive efforts by foster and adoptive parents. Educational difficulties had generally been underestimated prior to placement and new parents had a key role in identifying educational needs which had been undetected while the children were in care. At the start of the placements only a third of the 61 primary school age children were thought to need some form of remedial help, though this proportion had risen to over half by the end of the first year. Unfortunately, the level of provision did not match this need. Many parents thought their child was having difficulty translating their abilities into achievement at school and attributed this to: difficulty in grasping particular concepts (for example money or time), lack of age-appropriate basic skills (such as reading or writing), fear of failure, disruptive behaviour and lack of concentration. While they had been looked after, no such personalised assessments had been made.

Recognising the failures in the present system, Cleaver (1996) suggested that children need a champion who will fight for their interests in school. Triseliotis *et al* (1995) found people specifically designated as children's advocates had been no more effective in securing educational provision than had the social workers. On the whole, young people preferred people they already knew to work things out on their behalf.

Clarity about roles and effective contact with the school

In their inspection report, Ofsted and SSI reported that none of the local authorities had clearly identified the role of the carer concerning children's education. There was a heavy reliance on carers to promote children's educational interests but no guidelines on what this should entail. When carers took a keen interest, this was very much appreciated by the children and was to their considerable advantage. Their school attendance was actively promoted and they were able to engage fully in school activities. Appropriate facilities were provided in the care settings and educational achievements were valued. Examples included one foster carer who arranged for the child to take mock GCSEs in the foster home and another who implemented a reading programme, with guidance from the school. In one residential unit individual children were allowed to choose the member of staff who would take a direct interest in their education. However the report concludes that 'in the majority of cases carers did not engage with schools and children's educational progress and achievements were not usually acknowledged or encouraged' (Ofsted/SSI 1995).

A similar lack of specificity about the carers' role in relation to education emerged from the two surveys of the Statements of Functions and Objectives prepared by each Scottish children's home in accordance with the 1987 Residential Regulations (Borland 1992; Borland 1995). Only two out of five statements included any details of how contacts with schools should be maintained, usually simply stating that the key worker would attend parents' evenings. Only 15% mentioned any arrangements to enable children to complete homework, including the carers' availability to give encouragement or help. Reference to education was more often made in the statements from homes providing longer-term care, which is consistent with the Ofsted/SSI finding that carers in short-term placements seldom invested the time and energy in contact with schools.

The teachers interviewed by Berridge *et al* (1996) described residential staff as behaving in similar ways to uninterested parents, for example by not attending parents' evenings, sports days or school functions and failing to inform the school when children were sick. However residential staff said they only attended school functions if birth parents were not able to be present. They also felt they lacked the necessary information and authority to negotiate effectively with schools and acknowledged that contact was usually about problems rather than routine liaison.

Neither does it seem that field social workers necessarily take on the key role in liaising with schools or taking an interest in the children's education. The Ofsted/SSI report indicated that direct contact between social workers and schools was limited and irregular. Thus there were few opportunities to discuss the child's progress and share information which could affect the child's education. Schools were often unaware of important changes in the child's life, for example a change of placement, and so were unable to anticipate or understand unsettled behaviour.

The teachers interviewed by Berridge *et al* (1996) were more positive about contacts with social workers. Although more feedback would have been appreciated, they thought social workers were beginning to attach more importance to children's education.

Responsibilities of foster carers and social workers

As part of their study of the education of children in long-term foster care, Aldgate *et al* (1993) found that in the interests of normalisation, social workers generally preferred that carers maintained the day to day contact with school, while they themselves relied on reviews to monitor children's progress. Although the carers in this study were 'good parents' in terms of taking a personal interest in the children, maintaining contact with the school and providing a stimulating environment, the children were not able to overcome early educational disadvantage. This led the authors to conclude that children who are looked after need more than even the best parenting to succeed and that social workers may therefore need to be more proactive in linking with schools to identify what extra input might be needed. This supports Jackson's claim that more than average parenting is needed (Jackson 1995).

Fletcher-Campbell (1990) found that foster carers were good at liaising with schools but that back-up help was not available from social workers when they did not have the necessary experience or when the children had special needs. Quinton *et al* (1996) report similar lack of input from social workers in support of carers' attempts to secure extra resources.

Aldgate and colleagues compared social workers' and foster carers' views about responsibility for making key decisions regarding children's education (Aldgate *et al* 1993). They found a degree of discrepancy in that 90% of social workers but only 37% of carers expected that long-term plans for education would be made jointly between the social worker and carer. Three out of five carers expected that they alone would make decisions on long-term plans. Similarly, 80% of carers expected that it was their responsibility to choose the school for their foster child whereas most social workers expected to contribute to the decision.

Involving birth parents

Birth parents or others with parental responsibility are also potential key players in decision-making about children's education and should be encouraged to maintain links with the school. Under the Children (Scotland) Act 1995, local authorities have duties to consult with parents of looked after children and to take their views into account when making decisions which affect their child. They are also required to promote contact between children and parents and to prepare the child for when (s)he is no longer looked after. Promoting parents' links with the school would be consistent with implementing these duties but very little has been written on this topic.

Accounts of children brought up in care provide evidence of the importance of parental involvement. Jackson (1994) reported that for some of the educationally successful care-leavers in her study, contact with birth parents had helped sustain their motivation in difficult circumstances. She also cites the example of one young man who obtained a PhD in Applied Linguistics despite being assumed of low ability as a black child in care. Throughout his childhood in care, he maintained links with his father who played a significant role in fostering his belief in himself (Jackson 1989).

The Ofsted/SSI report (1995) indicated that insufficient attention was given in statutory reviews to the involvement of those with parental responsibility. Schools generally knew when contact with parents was to be avoided but seldom understood the importance of attempts to maintain parental responsibility. Thus schools did not keep parents informed of children's educational progress through school reports or invitations to parents' nights. They generally communicated with carers who did not always share relevant information with the parents. Ironically, residential staff often think that teachers should communicate directly with birth parents, but teachers are often unaware of this expectation (Berridge *et al* 1996). Evidently clarification is needed on all sides about school/parent/carer communication.

Parenting when children are excluded from school

The responsibilities of social workers and carers when children are excluded from school are also unclear. Ward (1995) suggests that a reasonable parent might see that they had a role to compensate if their children were out of school but social workers saw this as an educational responsibility. Less than a fifth of Statements of Functions and Objectives reviewed by Borland (1992) contained any details of the role of carers when children were excluded from school, though approximately half the homes had had at least one child excluded in the previous year (Harvey 1992). In summary, social work departments have some way to go to attain good parenting in relation to education. Key elements in changing practice are:

- a clear statement about the value of education
- guidelines and procedures to clarify expectations of staff at different levels
- appropriate in-service training on education
- developing skills in effective negotiation with schools.

Clarity is needed about which person(s) maintain contact with school and act as an advocate for the child. This point is emphasised by Berridge and Brodie (1998) who found care staff were not well informed about appeal procedures in relation to exclusion. They also reported minimal liaison between schools, homes and the educational welfare service. As the Ofsted/SSI (1995) report concluded: 'the responsibility for the oversight of the children's educational needs often falls between the bureaucracies of social services and education. In most cases, the lack of one person responsible for fulfilling the role of parent in continuously pressing for improvement and inculcating in the child the importance of education has a seriously detrimental effect'. Despite these difficulties, for some young people admission to care provides an opportunity to concentrate on school work and make progress. As noted in chapter six, regular attendance, support from carers and increased interest from teachers had contributed to a more positive school experience for some young people (Fletcher 1993; Triseliotis *et al* 1995).

Residential care and education

Approximately 2,000 children being looked after by local authorities in Scotland are living in residential care, half living in residential schools and half in units without schooling on the premises. Residential schools were discussed in the previous chapter. Here we consider the educational environment in residential units (also referred to as children's homes), most of whose residents are of secondary school age.

In recent years residential care has been in the public eye as a series of incidents of serious abuse and infringements of children's basic rights came to light (see for example Levy & Kahan 1991). In addition to reports into specific instances of abuse, high levels of public and professional concern prompted general inquiries into the operation of residential care in each part of the UK (Utting 1991; Skinner 1992). Similar themes emerged from all these reports, namely that residential care continued to be an important part of child-care provision but that the service had been under-resourced and changes were needed to meet present day demands. Key issues were lack of qualified staff, unsuitable buildings and lack of an appropriate range of resources resulting in children with very different needs and problems living together.

In Scotland the Skinner report (Scottish Office 1992) made 66 specific recommendations and established eight fundamental principles which were to underpin residential child-care. The principles were set out as follows:

1.   Individuality and Development
Young people and children in residential care have the right to be treated as individuals who have their own unique relationships, experiences, strengths, needs and futures, irrespective of the needs of other residents. They should be prepared for adulthood and supported until they are fully independent.

2.   Rights and Responsibilities
Young people, children and their parents should be given a clear statement of their rights and responsibilities. They should have a confidential means of making complaints. They should be involved in decisions affecting them and in the running of the home.

3.   Good Basic Care
Young people and children in residential care should be given a high standard of personal care. They should be offered new, varied and positive experiences of life and should be included in the wider community.

4.   Education

Young people and children should be actively encouraged in all aspects of their education, vocational training or employment and offered career guidance.

5.   Health

Young people's and children's health needs should be carefully identified and met; they should be encouraged to avoid health risks and to develop healthy lifestyles.

6.   Partnership with Parents

Young people and children in residential homes and schools should be cared for in ways which maximise opportunities for parents' continued involvement, and for care to be provided in the context of a partnership with parents, wherever this is in the interests if the child.

7.   Child-Centred Collaboration

Young people and children should be able to rely on a high quality of inter-disciplinary teamwork amongst the adults providing for their care, education and health needs.

8.   A Feeling of Safety

Young people and children should feel safe and secure in any residential home or school.

Since the publication of the Skinner report, the issue of safety in residential care has been further highlighted. In the report of the Scottish Office review of safeguards to protect children away from home, four key elements were identified: better recruitment arrangements; raising the professional status of carers, more information about what happens in homes and an open culture which does not tolerate abusive behaviour (Kent 1997). The review acknowledges that both carers and peers can present a serious risk but that abuse by peers is a more common occurrence.

In the literature review which accompanies Kent's report, Kendrick (1997) acknowledges that bullying within residential care has been given relatively little attention, in contrast to the extensive literature about such behaviour in schools. He reports however that evidence of bullying has emerged from several studies which were interested in children's experience in residential schools and homes (Grimshaw & Berridge (1994); Triseliots *et al* (1995); Buchanan *et al* (1993). In one project, the carers were not aware of the level of abuse from peers or the distress which this caused (Buchanan *et al* 1993). This may lend support to the concern expressed by Utting (1997) that a certain level of abuse and intimidation can become 'acceptable' within some institutional settings. As within schools, bullying is reduced in homes where an open, supportive ethos is encouraged and no abuse of power by staff or residents is tolerated.

The Skinner principles now provide a framework for evaluating the quality of residential child-care throughout Scotland. They give due prominence to educational matters, including an emphasis on health education. However broad principles do not in themselves provide instant solutions and the literature provides a fairly depressing picture of the capacity of children's homes to promote the educational opportunities of their young residents.

The educational environment of residential units

Several writers have commented on the ways in which living in a residential home limits children's educational opportunities. Writing in 1985, Berridge's observations indicated that life in a children's home was dull and unstimulating and that staff were preoccupied with domestic tasks rather than the development of the children. Colton (1988) observed that residential staff usually spent much less time with children than foster carers. Parker (1988) identified three key sources of difficulties: the character of the staff group, the conditions and style of life in children's homes and failure of liaison between homes and schools. A more recent study by Berridge *et al* (1996) focused primarily on these elements, providing valuable insight into the educational environment of present day children's homes. The researchers spent time in three homes in one authority, talking to staff and young people, formally interviewing staff and observing life in the home at different points in the day. They concluded that: 'In most aspects, it seemed that the standard being aimed at was to provide what could be expected of a reasonable parent, though it may be felt that, in some instances, a lower standard seemed to apply. Examples were observed of homes and their staff clearly feeling able to go beyond this standard to try to provide the extra input which would be required positively to compensate young people for their early disadvantage'.

Having already considered the crucial aspect of liaison with schools, here we focus on four other aspects of home life relevant to children's educational experience: suitable facilities for completing homework, staff's actions in promoting education, school-related daily routine, and culture and practice in relation to school non-attendance.

Suitable facilities for homework

The study by Berridge *et al* (1996) revealed commitment to ensuring that young people had a quiet place to do homework and some young people's own rooms were well-equipped with a desk, reading lamp and bookshelf. However, there was a general scarcity of books, newspapers and reference materials which might be needed to complete homework. One home had a computer but its use was somewhat restricted because of lack of staff expertise and suitable software.

Most staff appreciated the importance of homework and expressed a willingness to offer young people help but the researchers observed that more pressing demands could take up staff time so that the commitment to help with homework was not always reflected in practice. In one home, staff found it difficult to know whether the children had any homework and in no home was there an expectation that homework would be done at a specified time or before other activities were allowed.

In her case study of a children's home which set out to put education at the top of its agenda, Jackson stressed the importance of homework within their strategy. Considerable emphasis was placed on completing homework, an hour being set aside each evening during which two teachers were available to help any child in difficulty. In addition, the home's link teacher recruited outside volunteers to help. Jackson (1988–89) reported that being able to hand in acceptable pieces of work transformed children's attitudes towards going to school and also changed teachers' perceptions of their ability and potential. In chapter eight we include descriptions of similar schemes in South Lanarkshire and Inverclyde which involve link teachers helping with homework.

Despite these encouraging developments, young people have consistently reported a wish for better study space (Buchanan *et al* 1993; Fletcher 1993; Freeman *et al* 1993).

> 'I don't have much time to myself – there is always something happening eg an admission or a fight so I have no time to do homework.'
>
> 'There is kids that are always picking on me all the time when I try to do my homework.'   Fletcher 1993

Reported also in the same studies are young people requesting more interest and support from residential staff as regards schooling.

Staff's actions in promoting education

In the homes visited by Berridge and colleagues, staff placed a high value on informal interaction with the young people and there was a strong commitment to ensuring that someone was able to give attention to the children at all times. However the researchers noted that staff tended to be reactive rather than proactive in this, agreeing to do something with a young person if asked but seldom initiating activities. An impressive range of outings and holidays were organised but the educational potential of these was not always realised. Similarly, staff were 'companionable and passive' when watching television but did not use programmes to prompt wider discussion.

Again Jackson (1989) provides a contrasting description of how education in the broadest sense was 'woven into the fabric of daily life' at the home which she studied. Education was viewed as extending far beyond school work and children were encouraged to participate in local clubs, take up hobbies and become well-informed about the world and current affairs. At the community meeting, a topical issue would be introduced for debate after home issues had been dealt with. Children were being prepared to be competent, knowledgeable and confident in the wider world.

The same community meetings provided opportunities for children's achievements to be acknowledged. Though staff interviewed by Berridge and colleagues recognised the importance of praise and encouragement, they sometimes overlooked achievements when faced with more pressing demands. The Skinner report (1992) emphasised the importance of staff paying attention to homework, valuing education and giving praise and encouragement to young people. Recognising that pressures on staff may make this difficult, the report suggests that befrienders can play a useful role in this respect.

The Who Cares? Trust book-buying scheme is an example of another means of encouraging a more educationally rich environment for children in care (Bald *et al* 1995). In the participating local authorities, selected children living in residential and foster care were given vouchers to buy books for personal reading up to the value of £25. In addition, an adult supporter, usually a residential social worker or foster carer, undertook to spend some time reading with them for at least three 20-minute sessions each week. At the end of the project, care staff reported that other demands on their time had made it difficult to safeguard even this amount of time for reading. In addition only a few had managed to arrange a visit to a library. However most children had enjoyed the adult interest in their reading and were pleased to be able to keep the books for themselves.

School-related daily routine

In terms of the daily routine of the home, Berridge and colleagues found that all the homes were well geared to facilitating school attendance. There was a good understanding of schools' individual early morning routines and when young people needed to set off. This level of understanding and organisation contrasted with the picture given by Carlen *et al* (1992) of care staff forgetting to make transport arrangements, with the result that young people arrived at school late. The authors comment that being in trouble for events outwith their control did nothing to encourage attendance.

At the end of the school day, the Berridge team found staff making attempts to talk with the children about their day at school and pick up on any successes or worries, though again demands on time restricted their availability. They portray a different picture from that reported in earlier work by Berridge (1985) which showed staff giving priority to domestic tasks. For instance, the author provided a graphic account of a child coming home from school, bursting to recount the days events, 'only to find adult attention firmly focused on the chip pan and the frozen fishfingers'. Nowadays it seems that staff understand the need to give attention to the children, and try to provide it, but the demands of caring for a difficult group of children may produce the same result: showing interest in what happened at school takes second place to more pressing concerns.

Returning to their most recent study, the Berridge team found that staff did not pay a great deal of attention to checking that letters from school had been handed over nor to ensuring that young people had the equipment they needed for the next day, but children were encouraged to go to bed reasonably early so that they could get the best out of school the following day (Berridge *et al* 1996).

Culture and practice in relation to school non-attendance

One criticism frequently levelled at children's homes is that staff tacitly accept non-attendance at school, so that this becomes part of the culture to which new entrants are quickly introduced. As one young woman interviewed by Biehal *et al* (1995) said: 'in the end they just used to let us stay in bed… and not bother going to school… I used to be able not to go… I don't know why.' Four of the young people in Biehal's study first truanted when they entered residential care and all attributed this to pressure from their peers and a culture of non-attendance. With hindsight, some young people regretted that they had not been more effectively controlled but at the time their opposition to attendance had been strong, presenting staff with a difficult dilemma.

Berridge *et al* (1996) also reported that staff were unsure how to handle outright refusal to attend school and in a couple of cases this led to avoidance of the whole issue. Most staff were strongly committed to avoiding a culture of non-attendance but a significant minority seemed to adopt a more passive approach and one member of staff commented that truancy was to be expected.

Practice in relation to young people not attending school also varied. In two homes some clear principles had been established, for example that young people should be engaged in positive activities such as craft work, shopping or doing jobs around the house and should not be allowed to stay in bed or watch television. It could be difficult to implement even these basic principles since the reasons for young people being at home during the day varied widely and defining 'non-attendance' was more difficult than expected. In the third home, no clear expectations of non-attenders had been established.

An exclusive focus on attendance as opposed to attainment has been criticised but it is also acknowledged that regular attendance is generally a prerequisite for progress (Jackson 1989; Berridge *et al* 1996). A National Children's Bureau project in four authorities in the north of England seems to be demonstrating that addressing issues systematically within the staff group can have positive results. When the project began, no child was attending school in any of the four participating homes. The first stage of the project, which involved only 'team-building' within staff groups, resulted in an increase to 50% attendance. Following the establishment of core groups within each home, comprising care staff, children, young people who had previously been in care, educational psychologist and teacher, all residents were attending school (Sandiford, in preparation). This seems to highlight the importance of staff attitudes and inter-agency cooperation in relation to non-attendance.

Training and educational background of residential staff

The training of residential staff emerged as a priority in the various reports into the quality of care in children's homes. There is widespread agreement that caring for young people in residential care is a demanding task which requires a trained workforce with a wide range of skills and knowledge. In Scotland, the Skinner report recommended that all local authorities and independent organisations should aim to achieve a position in which 30% of all residential child-care staff and 90% of senior staff should hold a Diploma in Social Work or equivalent. In addition, 60% of staff should be assessed as competent at HNC/SVQ level 3 (Skinner 1992).

In relation to the education of children in care, there are two related but distinct ways in which staff's own educational background and training are considered relevant. Firstly, effective negotiation with schools and managing challenging behaviours such as non-attendance, require skill and confidence which untrained staff may not have. The residential workers interviewed by Berridge *et al* (1996) said they were unsure how to approach schools and they felt patronised by teachers because they had no qualifications. Qualified staff felt much more confident and there was a view that only senior staff were considered by teachers as fellow professionals. The staff also felt they lacked enough knowledge to advocate on behalf of children and would have liked more training on special education, the statementing process and the law.

The second way in which carers' educational background is considered important is that it influences their attitudes towards the importance of education (Jackson 1989). In a study of staff attitudes towards their own training nearly two decades ago, Millham *et al* (1980) found that only 32% of the group had enjoyed their own school days, 62% had failed their eleven plus examination and 59% had left school at 16 with limited qualifications. As managers working in residential child-care, they had done well with minimal qualifications. The importance of formal schooling was not borne out by their own experience so was unlikely to be seen as a priority. Bald *et al* (1995) also found that unhappy experiences in their own education led to some staff feeling inhibited about offering educational support or dealing with teachers.

Support services and integrated practice

While practices within residential units are clearly important, improving the educational environment of children's homes requires action outwith as well as within the homes. Policy statements which emphasise the value of education, clarity about the expectations of staff and an adequately resourced service are needed if staff are to be consistently proactive. At an individual level, social workers and teachers share responsibility for effective liaison between residential units and schools. Inter-agency collaboration is considered in more detail in chapter eight.

Foster care

Approximately half the children being looked after in Scotland live in foster care, of whom approximately two thirds are of primary school age (Scottish Office 1996a). Foster care is generally the preferred placement for children under 12 and has also been effective with teenagers (Downes 1992; Hill *et al* 1996). Some of the problems identified within residential care are considered to be lessened in foster care. Foster carers take a personal interest in the children they care for and the potentially negative and contaminating aspects of peer culture are largely avoided (Colton 1988).

The educational environment in foster care

There is indeed some evidence that children in foster care do better educationally than their peers in children's homes (though the homes tend to care for older and more 'difficult' children). Biehal *et al* (1995) found that those young people who did get qualifications had had intensive support from foster carers, having been encouraged, for example, to stay on at school for another year or to move into further education. Similarly Jackson (1994) reported that many of the educationally successful care-leavers in her survey spoke warmly about receiving support from foster carers who often advocated on their behalf with education and social services. Heath *et al* (1994) reported that the foster carers in their study had high expectations: only 10% thought the children should leave school at 16, almost two fifths expected children to stay on at school until 18 and a further 27% thought their children might go on to higher education. They were described as 'model parents' in terms of linking with the schools, encouraging children and providing an educationally rich environment, for example through outings. Quinton *et al* (1996) also report that parents in permanent substitute families devoted considerable energy to identifying children's educational needs and seeking appropriate remedial help. They also spent time helping with homework, some devising ingenious ways of engaging children's attention and helping them learn.

Triseliotis and Russell (1984) were less optimistic about the educational environment in foster care, reporting that the attainment of adults brought up in foster care was poor compared with the achievement of similar children who had been adopted or brought up in residential care. The authors attribute this to the low expectations of foster carers whose ambitions for the children they cared for were in line with their own relatively modest educational achievements. Jackson (1989) makes a similar point about foster carers' limited education and aspirations.

However, a recent survey of foster carers in Scotland indicates that while the proportion who have 'O' grades is less than the national average, the percentage having a degree is equal to that in the general population. In other words, foster carers are drawn from across the educational spectrum, though a substantial proportion have no formal qualifications (Triseliotis *et al* 1998a). One criticism of long-term foster care in the past was that children were unclear of their status or security in the family. Aldgate and colleagues found that educational progress in foster care was associated with an expectation that the placement would last throughout childhood (Aldgate *et al* 1993) Thus lack of security about the future may have contributed to the poor progress of people who had been in foster care in Triseliotis and Russell's (1984) sample.

Jackson (1989) suggests that training for foster carers should include more information on the curriculum, education system and how to work with schools. The National Foster Care Association's guide for foster carers provides this for carers in England and Wales (NFCA 1996). Information on relevant legislation and educational practice is included alongside guidance on how foster carers might support children's education within and outwith school. The requirements of children with special needs and care-leavers are specifically addressed.

A major study of the educational attainment of children in long-term foster care was carried out by Aldgate and colleagues (Aldgate 1992) (key findings are summarised on page 121.) Children in foster homes where at least one carer was educated to 'A' level did better on the reading and vocabulary tests than other foster children but did not make greater progress over time. The central finding of this research was that, even in stable foster placements which provided educationally rich environments, children were unable to overcome early educational disadvantage. The authors concluded that 'normal' family life and 'normal' parenting are not enough to compensate for earlier deprivation. Reading skills did improve when children received specialist help with reading but this was only offered to the children with the poorest academic performance. The authors suggest that these 'greater than average educational inputs' may be necessary for all children in care if they are to have an opportunity to realise their potential.

The PRAISE project in Salford (Menmuir 1994) is one example of providing 'greater than average educational input' in a way which involves carers and helps them engage young people in educationally enriching activities.

Residential and foster carers were trained to use specific reading strategies with children in their care in order to promote reading as an enjoyable activity as well as an essential skill. Three reading approaches were used: shared reading, partnered silent reading and paired reading. A training pack was developed and project staff advised carers on how to approach reluctant readers. A range of suitable and interesting books was provided. The project was evaluated through carers' weekly records which indicated that children were reading regularly and were enjoying it.

Summary

Social workers have been criticised for underestimating the importance of education and for failing to understand that a positive educational experience enhances self esteem and promotes social as well as academic progress. However there is evidence that attitudes are changing. Current legislation, policy and frameworks for good practice require that a high priority is accorded to the education of children looked after by the local authority.

Although for some young people admission to care provides an opportunity to concentrate on school work, being looked after often impacts adversely on young people's school experience primarily because:

– no-one takes a personal interest in their education
– there is lack of clarity about responsibilities among professionals
– changes of school become more frequent
– education is not valued in the care environment.

There is some evidence that residential staff increasingly appreciate the importance of education and seek to give appropriate support, but lack of confidence about educational matters, resource constraints and constantly having to deal with crises make this difficult in practice.

Foster care seems to provide a more educationally rich environment. However even where foster carers provide intensive educational support, it can be difficult for children to overcome earlier disadvantage, especially when they have been abused or are uncertain about their future. Additional educational inputs are needed, though generally scarce. A number of schemes which encourage reading have been developed.

8
Collaboration between Social
Work and Education

In the preceding two chapters the school and care systems have been examined separately. While this is probably a necessary step, the most salient message to emerge from young people, inspection reports and research is that progress is dependent on working across department boundaries. We now move on to examine how child-centred collaboration might point the way forward.

The value of close links between education and social work services was recognised in the Kilbrandon report (1964). Though Kilbrandon's far-sighted recommendations to set up the children's hearing system were accepted, the collaborative Social Education Departments envisaged were not established. Social work and education services developed separately, each department creating its own ethos and administrative systems which could impede rather then facilitate effective child-centred collaboration (Bruce 1987; Kendrick 1995c; Kendrick *et al* 1996). It might be argued that the Children (Scotland) Act 1995 provides a second chance to establish the close collaboration Kilbrandon envisaged. The requirement to compile children's services plans and to share responsibility provides an opportunity for local authorities to find new ways of working together 30 years after Kilbrandon's visionary recommendations were rejected.

It has been widely recognised that the poor educational experience of children in care is attributable in part to the fact that responsibility for their education falls into an uncertain zone between the two major bureaucracies of social work and education (Fletcher-Campbell & Hall 1990; Walker 1994). Jackson (1989) urged that in order to improve children's educational experience, cooperation was necessary at structural, practical and attitudinal levels. More recent research by Fletcher-Campbell (1997) and a current project by Who Cares? are reaching the same conclusion (Fletcher 1998).

In this chapter we outline key aspects of collaboration between education and social work, focusing on policy and service development, establishing collaborative structures and cooperating at case level. The evidence suggests that developing effective joint working is a difficult process which requires commitment at all levels of both services. It further highlights that improving the educational experience of children looked after away from home is not a discrete exercise but requires both social work and education to examine and adapt a range of established practices (Fletcher-Campbell 1997; Fletcher 1998). The message is that realising the spirit of Kilbrandon will require concerted effort by all concerned.

Policy and service development
England and Wales

A survey of English and Welsh local authorities in 1996 provides the most up to date indicator of developments in policy and practice (Fletcher-Campbell 1997, 1998). Comparing the results with those of a similar study undertaken almost a decade ago (Fletcher-Campbell & Hall 1990) the author concludes that progress has been made but that this is patchy so that the service individual children receive varies depending on where (s)he lives or the commitment of individual carers and teachers.

In terms of progress, there was far greater awareness of the fact that many children looked after away from home were receiving a poor education. There was also more understanding of the crucial relationship between care and education plans; while in practical terms, a number of initiatives to develop practice had been set up across England and Wales. However only twenty-five authorities indicated that a specific policy had been developed. Based on this and responses to other questions, it was estimated that thirty authorities were actively addressing the issue of the education of looked after children, though another twenty indicated they had plans to do so (Fletcher-Campbell 1997). This is despite the issuing of the joint circular in 1994 (DoE & DoH 1994) and widespread dissemination of key points from the report of the Ofsted/ SSI joint inspection (1995).

The requirement to produce corporate children's services plans might be expected to give an impetus to joint policy development though experience in England and Wales indicates that effective collaboration does not develop easily (Sutton 1995). While visionary plans may be written, translating them into practice requires adequate resources and commitment to grapple with difficult and inevitable tensions between the two departments (Fletcher 1998). A Scottish study on inter-disciplinary working also identified these tensions between departments, particularly in relation to budgetary matters (Kendrick *et al* 1996). The indications are that while developing children's services plans provides a framework within which service provision *may* be reshaped in a more collaborative way, this is not a guaranteed by-product.

In 1996, aware that effecting change based on collaboration is a complex and difficult process, the Gulbenkian Foundation and several other charitable trusts invited the Who Cares? Trust to establish an action research project. The aim of the Equal Chances project is 'to improve the educational experiences and achievements of children and young people in public care' by 'helping local authorities to become effective corporate parents'. Working beside staff in two English local authorities, project workers are facilitating the process of developing policy and structures conducive to better educational experiences (Fletcher 1998). The intention is that by highlighting common elements in the process, all agencies will be able to learn from the experiences of the two participating authorities.

The Scottish perspective

Our contact with Scottish local authorities towards the end of 1996 indicated that only a few had specific policies in relation to the education of children in care, though many informed us that a system for collaboration between education and social work was in place and that principles of inclusion and maximising each child's educational opportunity would guide practice. Several provided details of joint policies which aimed to keep children in the community and within mainstream education. Five referred to a specific policy and/or service development on the education of children looked after. Here we provide a brief outline of developments in two areas.

South Lanarkshire: Educational Support Service for Children in Care

Work carried out in the Lanarkshire area shows a growth in measures established to promote the educational needs of looked after children. Practice dates back to 1985, when a framework aimed specifically to instigate positive discrimination for children in residential care was introduced in the Hamilton district of the former Strathclyde Region. This has centred on the provision of two link teachers and the introduction at district level of regular meetings of social work and education officers and educational psychologists. From the outset, the ethos of collaboration has been central.

The link teacher's role is to support young people in mainstream schooling. Upon entry into care, information on the young person is gathered, assessed and shared with each agency in order to maintain or locate the best educational placement. This process focuses on collaboration between social work staff, psychological services, the Reporter's department and parents.

The individualised role of link teachers is identified at a post-admission meeting and, in turn, is negotiated with schools or other educational establishments. In the school, the link teacher is involved in cooperative and individual teaching for the pupil and liaises with school management and teaching staff. In the children's home, tuition is given to young people awaiting placement, whilst staff are informed about the school curriculum and encouraged to become involved in the schooling process. Hence, the link teacher performs a dual function: ensuring that the child is able to make best use of education and generating effective collaboration between care and education staff. In the spirit of promoting collaboration, a joint staff development meeting has been organised to offer training to staff not involved in the original scheme. This has attracted interest from children in care staff, secondary school staff, primary headteachers and career service personnel.

These developments helped inform the Skinner Report which highlighted the valuable role link teachers perform and recommended the use of educational plans for all young persons in care. In South Lanarkshire the educational plan is well integrated with the overall care plan that is recorded in a separate user-friendly booklet. There are four main aims in developing an education plan. Firstly, it aids joint planning by coordinating information from the social worker, headteacher, link teacher and care staff. The second aim is to involve young people and their parents in education planning and consequently they are invited to all relevant meetings. A third aim is to develop a framework of realistic goals in accordance with individual needs. This may highlight that remedial assistance or a gradual build-up of attendance is required. The plans encompass a broad definition of education so that social, practical, creative and physical activities are considered as well as literacy, numeracy and other academic skills and knowledge. A fourth and overall aim is to boost the young person's educational attainments and self-esteem. Currently, support plans cover only those in residential care but, at the time of writing (March 1998) South Lanarkshire was about to re-launch the scheme, with the intention of integrating children in foster care into the process. It is envisaged that this should take place within the next twelve months (personal communication).

Initiatives have also emerged to provide support beyond the care stage and towards independent living. In order to maintain a similar level of inter-agency support at the school leaving stage, a joint working group has been set up to consider issues dominating the experience of care-leavers entering the job market (such as low educational attainment and unemployment). Again, participants include representatives from education and social work but with additional input from community education career services, further education colleges and training agencies. In addition it is emphasised that the opinions of young people taking part in the Through-Care Services Report are directly included in this process. As with most local initiatives, formal evaluation of practice has yet to develop. However, available figures indicate that at least 75% of young people in children's units have a support plan and staff in Hamilton District believe that this resulted directly in their having the lowest proportion of children in residential schools in Strathclyde (personal communication).

The Inverclyde Children's Units Support Project

Support for children in designated residential units began in Inverclyde in November 1995. The remit was to provide support for children in care but only those in residential care are included in the project, although foster care is currently under examination by the team (personal communication). As there are very few teenagers in foster care in the area this has not become a prioritised concern. Given that no exact specifications were set, considerable flexibility has been built into the project work. Akin to work in South Lanarkshire, the project uses a link teacher to liaise between children's units and schools in providing focused educational and emotional support to the child. The aim is both to increase attainments and help gain access to jobs and training opportunities. Again, joint planning between schools and children's units is central with direct emphasis on helping the young person and on assisting residential staff to create an educationally rich environment.

Unlike South Lanarkshire where link teaching is funded from the social work budget, Inverclyde receives funding from the Inverclyde Regeneration Trust. Original financial backing came from Urban Aid. More recently, the Inverclyde Project compiled a report including an application to extend the service to cover support in mainstream education after young people return home. This has been matched with a push to complete education plans for more children. Implicit in this is recognition of the need to develop links with schools so that plans are held and owned by the school, thus ensuring resources are provided (personal communication). Also in the application was a bid for more funds from the Inverclyde Regeneration Partnership. The project is managed jointly by the Education and Social Work departments.

It took some time for the project to become fully operational as the link worker had to build up relationships with a variety of teaching staff and to establish a role within each school. However, early assessment of the project has shown a number of positive outcomes. The link teachers' advocacy role has proved particularly helpful, notably when dealing with pupil exclusion and reintegration into schools. Moreover, residential and field social workers believe that a major contribution has been the facilitation of a learning culture within residential units. Individualised educational support for young people has been developed through programmes set up by the link teacher and managed by children's home staff in her absence. Staff see this as in stark contrast to the former educational isolation of young people in care. In turn, the support provided by the project has enabled some young people to return to, and remain in, mainstream education. This contrasts with a pre-project situation, where practitioners contend that young people would have been far more likely to end up in a residential school (personal communication).

Since 1997, a more detailed assessment of the project has indicated a growing overall number of Standard Grade passes and far fewer exclusions. There is evidence of increased support for the children, both in terms of the educational environment in homes, (for example, through wider availability of computers and funding to buy a stock of past exam papers) and by close monitoring of school work by the link teacher. For example, the link teacher monitors homework two nights a week, allowing problems to be picked up and dealt with before creating difficulties in school. Thus the project has aimed to integrate a preventative approach. Furthermore, the link teacher provides career support – the success of this may be equated with an increased number staying on at college (personal communication).

In the course of this review we also received information about initiatives in other parts of Scotland. They include the Children in Care Joint Support Project funded by Urban Aid in Renfrewshire. Similar to work carried out in South Lanarkshire and Inverclyde, this provides additional educational support for children in local authority children's residential units through the appointment of two teachers. Support initiatives are also currently being developed in Midlothian. Here service provision integrates a more external approach to learning support through using psychologists to provide initial assessment and then teaching support from a team of outreach teachers. Work carried out in Dumfries and Galloway has centred on surveying the health and education needs of children in care by collating information from parents and schools. It was envisaged that this information would be used to pinpoint specific areas of difficulty and frame appropriate service responses (personal communication).

Key elements of effective policy

The Equal Chances project (Fletcher 1998) has identified three key stages in the process of developing an effective collaborative policy. First it is necessary to map the educational needs of children within the authority. Information about the educational experience and attainment of looked after children is not collated routinely, so that for most authorities identifying the nature and extent of the problem is a necessary first step. Fletcher warns that this has proved a difficult exercise, partly due to incompatibility of computer systems but also because it involves confronting how the system has been letting children down. The exercise may result in the development of joint management-information systems between social work and education, in itself a major step towards establishing trust and cooperation.

The second element is to look at what each school has to do differently, involving young people in this process as fully as possible. How to handle information about individual pupils is one example of a policy which needs to be developed at school level. Inevitably, there is a tension between identifying children as entitled to special consideration and respecting their wishes for confidentiality. The approach of the project is to enable schools to develop ways of working which include consultation with young people about the setting up of such systems and allow individual young people to participate in decisions about which information (about them) should be disclosed. Fletcher (1998) reports that both social workers and teachers found it surprisingly difficult to open up this kind of discussion with young people and were pleased to have the support of project staff to begin the process. It is hoped that in time it will become routine.

The third stage is for the authority to set targets for change, based on the specific problems identified by the initial mapping of need. Priorities will thus be different for each authority, so that one, for example, may focus on exclusion rates while others will aim to improve attainment or attendance. Progress can then be monitored regularly. Joint training or the creation of particular posts may be means of reaching the required standard.

Fletcher identifies partnership, prevention and equal treatment as three key principles which should underpin these developments. Partnership involves staff at all levels of social work and education knowing about each other's roles and expectations but also involves talking to children and parents and keeping elected members informed about developments. Good collaboration should aim to prevent young people being further disadvantaged within the care system and should ensure that they have the same educational opportunities as their peers.

Fletcher-Campbell (1997) identifies a similar ethos as necessary for effective collaboration and, in terms more usual in relation to special needs education, suggests that policies should be informed by three key concepts: integration, inclusion, and progression. Distinguishing between 'integration' and 'inclusion', she uses 'integration' to refer to situations in which a child with special needs is being introduced into an existing environment, requiring adaptation by the child and/or the school. Inclusion, on the other hand, focuses on creating environments which are able to accommodate the diverse needs of those using a particular service.

Applying these concepts to the education of looked after children, Fletcher-Campbell highlights three aspects of integration. First, she points out that children who have become accustomed to a chaotic lifestyle and have not been attending school need a transitional period during which gradual integration takes place. Thus schools may need to allow time for children to become accustomed to school life, perhaps through part-time attendance and gradual introduction to the school routine. Second, the concept of integration applies at an individual level. Young people's lives need to be 'personally integrated' with the recognition that education and care are part of a whole life and that changes in one has consequences for the other. Close cooperation between services is the third element. Identifying the obstacles to joint working at policy level, she recognises that social services and education departments have very different priorities and ways of conceiving of clients. The former deals with 2% of the school population and is relatively resource-intensive, while the latter deals with all pupils and resources are spread widely.

Collaboration between social services and education is also essential to creating 'inclusive' environments in schools. Fletcher-Campbell makes the point that staff in both need to have a shared understanding that looked after children are entitled to the same educational experiences as they would have had if family problems and abuse had not disrupted their lives. The professionals have a responsibility to create an environment which allows children and young people to learn: 'it is a matter of removing some of the burdens from these young people, despite the fact that the hard everyday reality is that many of these young people present as 'burdens' to schools'.

In terms of progression, Fletcher-Campbell advocates that a focus on educational progress should be built in. The aim should be not simply to ensure attendance or containment but to focus on achievement on a day by day, week by week basis. Particular attention to progress is needed at key stages, for example the transition from primary to secondary or when making choices about options in the later stages of secondary school.

Both Fletcher-Campbell and Fletcher emphasise strongly that a whole-authority approach is needed. While time-limited projects can demonstrate that progress can be made, most benefits will be lost shortly after the project ends unless change takes place in both social work and education systems. There needs to be commitment and change at all levels from elected members to front-line staff, with clearly defined policy statements setting out the authority's aims and what is expected of staff. Emphasising that each part of the system has a part to play, Fletcher-Campbell (1998) provides the following chart of the individuals or organisations who can be expected to have an impact at the national, local, institutional and individual levels.

National: Department of Health, Department for Education & Employment, Social Services Inspectorate, Her Majesty's Inspectors of Schools, national voluntary organisations

Local: Social services department (senior and middle managers) Local education authority (officers, advisers, inspectors) Elected members
Voluntary organisations
Head teachers association
Education support services
Education psychology service
Youth service
Foster carers support groups

Institutional: Teachers, residential workers, peripatetic support staff, special project staff

Personal: Teachers, carers, support staff, birth parents, siblings, peers and other pupils

Given that so many people are involved, structures for implementing policy become crucial.

Structures for collaboration

As responses from around the country indicated, the primary aim of collaboration between social work and education in Scotland has been to keep children within mainstream education and out of care. From an educational perspective, joint working has been viewed for some time as essential to the teaching of children with emotional and behavioural difficulties. Writing about inter-agency approaches in this complex field, McKay (1994) asserts: 'No single body or interest can be expected to resolve the issues which can arise. It is, therefore, essential that all potential partners are committed to working together throughout the process of supporting young people. These processes range from early identification, assessment and intervention to remedial action, placement in care and, at the end of the continuum of provision, possible residential placement'.

There has been some debate about the most appropriate location of responsibility for looked after children within the education structure. Despite official reluctance that this be subsumed under responsibilities for children with special educational needs (DoE & DoH 1994), some commentators have pointed out that, in practice, the necessary skills and resources are often to be found among special needs staff. Thus, in the absence of a specific service for children looked after, the special needs teacher is often called upon (Fletcher-Campbell, 1997).

Barr (1994) makes the point that wherever specific responsibility for children with particular needs is located, structures have to facilitate cooperation at all levels of the organisation: 'Much of the success of the policy will depend on the extent to which separate services (for example education and social work) can adopt an integrated approach and negotiate separate contributions. This needs clear recognition and support both politically and administratively, for instance through a joint authority committee charged with coordinating and overseeing the policy implementation'.

This is echoed by Fletcher-Campbell (1997) and Fletcher (1998). They consider it critical that joint policies should be owned by the authority and implemented via multi-agency groups established at various levels within the authority.

During the 1980s joint youth strategies were developed in several Scottish local authorities. In a study of integration of residential child-care carried out in the early 1990s, Kendrick (1995a) outlined the operation of these strategies in three regions. In two instances the focus was primarily to keep individual children out of residential school, while the third adopted a wider community development approach. Young people's difficulties were viewed in the context of changing social relationships and deprivation, the strategy aiming to be relevant to all young people and to involve a range of community agencies.

However, even within these joint policies, educational needs can be marginalised. By giving priority to 'prevention' some young people may find themselves no longer eligible for 'preventive' resources after they go into care (Francis 1997). Neither will the needs of looked after children necessarily be addressed within systems for children with emotional, behavioural or learning difficulties (Fletcher-Campbell 1997). Writing about the development of the Manchester Teaching Service, Walker (1994) pointed out that the interests of children looked after by local authorities cut across departmental boundaries. These children do not necessarily have emotional and behavioural difficulties but often require a rapid and flexible educational response which may be incompatible with the structure and organisation of special educational needs services. Walker considers that the Manchester service was significant in bridging the structural divide between social services and education because its overall objective was 'to ensure that education plays its fullest part in realising the policy objectives of the social services committee'. He viewed structural issues as critical: 'This is less specifically concerned with the educational performance of children within the local authority care system than it is a recognition of the interdependency of education and social work objectives. It acknowledges in structural terms that education is inextricably interwoven in the many crises, difficulties and traumas which create the need for social services intervention with children and young people'.

In her most recent research, Fletcher-Campbell (1997) conducted case studies in six local authorities which had developed a discrete education support service for looked after children, similar to those in Manchester, South Lanarkshire and Inverclyde. Based on interviews with young people, carers and a wide range of education and social work staff, she concluded that these services formed a vital link between education and social services. Among the key points about these services were the following:

- arrangements for funding varied across authorities and the nature of services reflected local circumstances and need
- having established a discrete education support service, policies, procedures and documentation had undergone rapid evolution
- the separate services saw themselves as mediators between education and social services departments. The ability to move with ease between social work and education were key skills for staff in specialist support services
- specialist staff were keen to assist schools and carers in supporting young people and did not offer long-term direct support to any individual young person. They engaged in formal training of colleagues across agencies and engaged in a range of supportive initiatives such as homework clubs

– most services focused on adolescents, though referrals of primary school age children were increasing

– the accessibility and responsiveness of the services were much appreciated by carers and teachers.

Within South Lanarkshire the success of the education support programme is partly attributed to the establishment of a core group of workers at local level to plan and deliver the service. The group is made up of the educational psychologist, a child-care manager from the social work department, two link teachers employed by the education department and an officer in charge from one of the children's homes. Thus the group makes links between social work and education at managerial level and across front-line staff (personal communication).

Evidently, key groups of this kind can only operate effectively within wider structures which promote collaboration. Writing about systems established to put youth strategies into operation, Kendrick (1995b) provides the following example from one Scottish authority:

Level One – Contact: involves individual agency staff working with a young person although attention is also to be paid to improving coordination and collaboration.

Level 2 – Networking: involves facilitation of inter-worker communication in respect of an individual child or young person with a view to addressing issues early and effectively yet informally.

Level 3 – Case Conference: is intended to address formally the identified problems of the child or young person with the appropriate professionals and resource managers, to determine the course of action.

Level 4 – Resource Management Group: receives case information from Level 3 and determines appropriate options. Involves staff at assistant director level and can identify additional resources, refer to off-site education or refer to Level 5.

Level 5 – Joint Directorate Executive: determines appropriate courses of action and decides on special measures extending exceptionally to residential care or education.

In addition, a monitoring system was set up, especially to focus on children who moved through stage five and were approaching residential provision.

Kendrick found that the setting up of structures did not, in itself, lead to policy implementation which remained patchy at school level. Though referred to by different names, a central feature of policy in each region was the school-based inter-agency liaison group. Not all schools had a liaison group and, even when there was one, its effectiveness was much influenced by the attitude of headteachers (Kendrick 1995c). Even within social work areas teams, there was a great deal of variation in the relationship between social workers and secondary schools. In addition, cooperation became more difficult as the process moved up the hierarchy. Kendrick *et al* (1996) concluded that: 'The success in getting policy agreed has not been matched to the same extent in all local areas and this has been attributed to a failure on both sides – social work and education – to give greater priority to working together and committing resources to joint strategies.

Several writers comment that effective cooperation presents a considerable challenge in the present climate of limited resources and market pressures (Jackson 1994). Based on research in a London borough, Sinclair *et al* (1994) reported that the ability to work together was hampered by arguments over budgeting and contracting. Similar problems were reported by Kendrick within the Scottish system. Only four of 34 residential school placements made during the study year were jointly funded and arguments over who should pay centred on whether school or other problems predominated. This was a matter frequently raised by children's panel members who felt that the best interests of the child could be lost in battles over financial responsibility. It remains to be seen whether the corporate responsibilities for children embodied in the Children (Scotland) Act 1995 will overcome some of these tensions or whether budgetary stresses will make them worse.

Barriers to joint working

One message which emerges clearly from the literature is that effective joint working requires more than developing appropriate policies and establishing systems and structures to implement them. When it comes to cooperating in the interests of individual children, the expectations and attitudes of front line staff are crucial. In a relatively recent study, Berridge and Brodie (1996) reported that though managers had a good shared understanding, field staff cooperated less effectively in practice.

The differing attitudes and perspectives of teachers and social workers have been well documented (Bruce 1987; Fletcher-Campbell & Hall 1990; McCullogh 1991; Bullock 1993). Writing in 1987, Bruce likened the study of the interface between social work and education to anthropological analysis of two very different cultures whose knowledge of each other is based as much on hearsay and assumption as on fact. It might be argued that there has been progress in collaboration in the last ten years but more recent studies have highlighted continuing lack of understanding on both sides.

While teachers may be ill-informed about social work planning processes and legal responsibilities (Ofsted / SSI 1995), social workers are said to have little understanding of the curriculum or teaching methods (Fletcher-Campbell 1991). As a result, Fletcher-Campbell argued that negotiations about school are more usefully handled by link teachers or psychologists whose bridging role equips them to understand and talk the language of both systems.

One key difference in attitudes centres on the relative priority attached to educational and social factors by the two professions. Fletcher-Campbell (1990a) is critical of social workers who put too much emphasis on 'whether children would fit in' and were not interested in what they would be learning. On the other hand, Bullock and colleagues conclude that teachers have no concept of the process of 'settling in' so that when children moved school on returning home from care, only their educational needs were considered (Bullock *et al* 1993). The joint inspectorate report also concluded that 'teachers and social workers do not understand the requirements of care and education respectively with the result that there is little discussion of the educational needs of children' (Ofsted/ SSI 1995).

McCullogh (1991) points out that teachers and social workers may use different models to explain difficult behaviour or slow learning. While teachers look for explanations primarily in terms of individual or family reasons, social workers may want also to consider environmental factors, including the impact of the school system. In a similar vein, social workers may view schools as having a welfare function while many teachers define their role largely in terms of teaching (Kendrick 1995c).

The two professional groups may also have different ideas about how or when to intervene most effectively. Fletcher-Hall (1990) notes that social workers favour a 'minimal intervention' approach and are wary of labelling children unnecessarily while teachers prefer early warning and action. Social workers are concerned for the individual child, but the teacher has to balance that concern with the needs of a whole class or group (Ofsted/ SSI 1995). It has also been noted that social workers and teachers may have a different understanding of confidentiality and that teachers might be frustrated when social workers do not share personal information about a child (Berridge *et al* 1996). Young people themselves have expressed concerns about information at school not being kept private (Gallagher 1996; Ofsted/ SSI 1995).

Fletcher-Campbell (1990) points out that simply working together does not bring social workers and teachers closer to understanding each other. Boundaries can in fact be reinforced with problems being seen as belonging to one department or the other. Joint training which encompasses examination of attitudes and values may be needed to prevent professional differences from blocking the development of truly child-centred services. The joint inspection report (Ofsted/ SSI 1995) noted that time and training needed for sound inter-agency collaboration is rarely reflected in the management priorities of either the care or the education system. Berridge and Brodie (1998) provide a powerful illustration of how the lack of clear policies and joint working arrangements impact on individual children.

Collaboration in relation to individual children

The final section of this chapter outlines the disappointing evidence that, in many areas, collaboration in relation to individual children remains ineffective.

Care planning

The Ofsted / SSI report indicated that the views of local education authorities and schools were seldom taken into account in pre-placement planning, leading to insufficient priority being given to educational arrangements for children. Schools contributed their views in only two out of eighteen cases and their opinions appeared to be given little weight by social work staff. Initial care planning was undertaken principally by social services staff in conjunction with adults with parental responsibility. The focus was primarily on the child's placement needs and there was little evidence that social service departments appreciated the importance of systematically including schools' views in planning. No doubt the general scarcity of choice in placements limited the extent to which other factors could be taken into account (Triseliotis *et al* 1995).

The Ofsted / SSI inspectors further reported that school files did not include care plans providing information on what action the school should take and that schools were sometimes unaware of plans for future placements and so could play no part in helping prepare the child. Where care plans did exist, they did not cover the tasks and responsibilities of all the interested parties, nor time scales nor the resource implications of educational decisions.

It is difficult to know whether similar findings would apply equally in Scotland. It might be argued that providing school reports for the children's panel hearing is a mechanism through which schools can influence key decisions directly. The study in Lothian carried out by Francis *et al* (1995) did not comment directly on the influence of school staff on pre-placement and early planning but did report that school staff were active participants in the reception into care process in relation to 28% of their admissions during 1992 and 38% of admissions in 1994.

Child-care reviews

Francis and colleagues also examined how schooling was addressed within child-care reviews. They found that educational matters were discussed at most initial reviews but raised questions about the detail and quality of that discussion, since an educational representative was present at only about a third. Education remained on the agenda at subsequent reviews but a member of school staff was present at only a quarter of these. Teaching staff were more likely to attend reviews of children in residential schools than those in foster care.

The Ofsted / SSI inspection reported that, in some authorities, teachers regularly attended or sent reports to statutory review meetings. However school staff were unsure what was expected from them and were often unclear about how reviews differed from other meetings such as child protection conferences or planning meetings. Schools were also given too little notice of meetings. In relation to children subject to a statement of special educational needs, there was little evidence of coordination between the two review systems.

Fletcher-Campbell (1990) criticised the much greater focus at reviews on attendance or behaviour rather than academic attainment and progress, pointing out that this conveys to the child that these are of little concern. She echoed the Ofsted / SSI finding that teachers were not always clear about the purpose of the review or what information they would need. This led her to question whether teachers need to be present at reviews, pointing out that they do not need to know the details of a child's circumstances to be supportive and that educational matters can be considered elsewhere. Young people themselves have also expressed disquiet at teachers being present when family or personal matters are discussed (Triseliotis *et al* 1995). On the other hand, Aldgate *et al* (1993) reported that social workers relied on reviews to monitor educational progress. Again we return to the need to collaborate in ways which suit individual children, operating within a framework which ensures that educational matters are not lost and that young people's needs for education and care are considered together.

There is frequent criticism in the literature of the failure to synchronise care and education plans (Fletcher-Campbell & Hall 1990; Bullock *et al* 1993). Moves of placement in the middle of term or shortly before exams can have dire consequences for the children concerned. Saddington (1988) recounts being moved to a placement 20 miles away two weeks before taking exams with the result that he left care with no qualifications.

One of main aims of the *Looking After Children* system, described in chapter seven, is to ensure that plans for children take account of all aspects of their lives (Parker *et al* 1991; Ward 1995). The system provides a framework which encourages discussion among all those sharing responsibility for a child and builds in close monitoring of progress. However, effectiveness of the system remains dependent on the actions of the professionals responsible for children's care, the 'corporate parents'. Experience in England and Wales shows that concerted effort is needed to change long-standing practices (Ward 1995).

Summary

It is now generally acknowledged that effective collaboration between education and social work staff at all levels is a prerequisite for improving educational experience and attainment. It is becoming equally apparent that establishing structures and practices which facilitate joint working requires considerable effort and commitment. While certain principles can guide the process, each authority has to develop a policy and strategy suited to its own needs. Most recent developments indicate that young people looked after away from home should be involved in this process. Furthermore, the longer-term value of short-term pilot projects is questionable unless they are able to influence practice within mainstream systems.

In Scotland, a few authorities have begun to develop policies and services concerned with the education of looked after children and South Lanarkshire has over a decade of experience. The requirement to produce children's services plans encourages local authorities to reshape policy and practice jointly, while in many authorities the introduction of the *Looking After Children* materials has the potential to increase collaboration in relation to individual children. Focused strategies will nevertheless be needed to ensure that long-standing tensions emanating from structural separation, attitudinal differences and territorial disputes do not present insurmountable barriers to staff from social work and education working together. Initiatives such as those in Inverclyde and South Lanarkshire provide grounds for optimism.

9

Implications for Policy, Practice and Research

The format and content of this review inevitably reflects the current level of understanding, planning and activity in relation to the education of children who are looked after by the local authority. As we have pointed out, publications which focus exclusively on this are confined to a handful of research studies, the joint circulars and inspection report and some reports of special initiatives. This literature charts the emergence of a recognised problem, attempts to understand its causes and begins to suggest ways of tackling it. The decision to include only British writing means that most works cited were written in the last ten years and come from England. While the differences between the Scottish and English education and child-care systems have to be borne in mind and reduce the direct applicability of this literature, the messages which emerge point clearly to ways in which educational provision for these children and young people could be improved.

So far, we have outlined the evidence that there is a problem to be addressed, examined the policy context and considered young people's experience at school and within the care system. We have also looked at recent developments in collaborative policy and practice and identified what needs to be in place to deliver an effective child-centred service. This concluding chapter provides an opportunity to summarise the main points and to explore some of the wider issues which may promote or inhibit progress. It ends by highlighting the problems and inter-relationships we need to understand more fully in order to provide the most appropriate support for individual children.

The educational situation of 'looked after' children

Most young people admitted to residential or foster care are already disadvantaged educationally. They then have to cope with the upheaval of leaving their home and the many losses that entails. Once in care, some aspects of their lives may improve but they have also to contend with the deficiencies of the care system outlined in this report. These include:

• the likelihood of further changes of placement and school
• a sense of stigma and concerns about confidentiality in school
• the marginality of education when key care decisions are made

- lack of clear responsibility amongst carers, parents and field social workers for educational support, liaison and advocacy
- carers' lacking skills, time or inclination to develop learning opportunities.

At school, few additional supports are available to help young people through the often multiple changes they face. The sense of being different can be an obstacle to learning, whilst alienation can engender behaviour difficulties or non-attendance. All too often the end result is a negative cycle of interaction between educational and care careers, especially for those in longer-term care without a stable placement. Yet for some individuals school works out well. Learning can be a life-line which enables young people to feel good about themselves and cope with other painful aspects of their lives. For others, being looked after confers the stability to attend school regularly for the first time and carers' encouragement spurs them on. Academic and non-academic achievements, personal support from teachers and peers can each be vital ingredients in enabling children to develop resilience to offset or overcome adversity. Specialist learning support and individualised programmes have been found to be effective in enabling some youngsters to turn around established patterns of underachievement or behaviour difficulties.

The potential significance of school thus cannot be overstated: it offers opportunities for academic attainment, improved self esteem and social support. This review has highlighted what needs to be in place to increase the likelihood that potential benefits will be realised. From young people themselves we learn that the key ingredients are a supportive school environment and sensitive arrangements for individual pupils. A school culture which welcomes diversity, fosters peer and staff support and does not tolerate bullying, helps children feel valued and supported and promotes the kind of trust which allows specific learning or social needs to be openly addressed. Both academic and emotional needs need to be catered for. Young people want teachers to focus primarily on their education, while being well informed of the ways in which their current circumstances may affect how they work and learn. They warn against the dangers of making assumptions or stereotyping and emphasise that each child who becomes looked after has individual needs and preferences. Consulting each pupil is thus essential.

The second essential element is close cooperation between school and welfare services. Policies and organisational frameworks need to support effective collaboration but the actions of front-line social workers and teachers are crucial for individual children. Teachers and social workers often have little awareness and understanding of each other's domains, which hampers effective communication. Each needs to be willing to seek out ways of supporting the work of the other: the teacher becoming involved in planning and offering support before, during and on return from a care episode; the social worker taking full account of the child's educational requirements at each stage, based on having sound understanding of his or her individual circumstances and needs. This kind of cooperation may help sustain existing arrangements and thus avoid unnecessary moves or, when moves are unavoidable, may help to ensure that they entail maximum support and minimum disruption for the child.

Implications for policy and practice

A clear message from the literature is that the barriers to young people's progress lie primarily in the care and education systems – and in the interaction between them. Several guides and policy documents now outline what is needed to change this, although research also indicates gaps between ideals and practice. One of the key elements is that social work and education should communicate effectively and share responsibility at all levels. Collaborative policies and mechanisms are needed at strategic, management and case levels, embracing education/social work interaction with regard to geographical areas, schools, care placements and individual children.

Findings from research and inspections indicate that at each of the four levels identified by Fletcher-Campbell (1997), there should be the following:

National

- guidance on good practice issued to local authorities

Local Authority

- accurate information obtained about the needs and situation in each authority
- corporate policies and action plans developed for the education of children looked after away from home
- management systems in place to monitor progress and identify changes, especially when children move school
- children's services plans identifying the educational needs of children looked after away from home and resources in place or required to meet them
- managerial responsibility for the education of looked after children established in departments of social work and education, with close cooperation between the designated officers

Institution

School:

- staff are aware of agency policy and practice in relation to looked after children
- a member of staff designated in each school with responsibility for overseeing the needs of the children

- a system established for ensuring quick transfer of information and individual support when children change school
- a system established for assessing whether additional help is needed
- a system developed for agreeing with the young person how information about their care status and needs is best handled within the school

Residential/ Foster Home:
- carers are aware of the authority's policy and expectations in relation to the education of children who are looked after away from home
- the home is well equipped with the resources needed for homework, eg reference books, computers, quiet space
- carers are well informed about school practice and curriculum
- carers talk to children about school and encourage them in their learning
- the ethos and routines of the home promote attendance at school and convey that education in important

Individual
- social workers, carers and teachers cooperate to ensure that educational needs are taken into account when planning for children
- education is given a high priority at child-care reviews
- young people's views are taken into account in all matters which affect their education

(The LAC assessment and action records can assist with all of these.)

Clearly these collaborative mechanisms need to be underpinned by education and social work staff having a better understanding of each other's responsibilities, priorities and ways of working.

At local authority level, the Children (Scotland) Act 1995 ought to provide an impetus to these developments. In particular, it requires that departments should collaborate and places a duty on all of them to promote and safeguard children's welfare. However there are also potential conflicts and tensions as education and social work services strive to conserve and maximise the use of limited resources. In addition, there is likely to be wide variation across the – generally smaller – local authorities which resulted from local government reorganisation. Joint guidance on the responsibilities of each department for the education of children in care would be helpful and could be fostered at a national level.

For schools, the literature highlights the importance of having a range of resources available which can be matched to individual needs and preferences. It is recommended that being looked after should qualify children for additional teaching if their attainment is below average and that an appropriate level of emotional support should be available, including intensive help at times of crisis. Secondary schools should help the child to identify a key support teacher.

On the social-care side, foster carers, residential staff and field social workers need training and time to ensure that the child's education is valued. Establishment policies, individual care plans and training should stress that attention be paid to homework, achievement and the development of educationally rich environments. Teachers have a clear role in advising on the kind of materials and activities which would be most appropriate.

For individual children, it is clear that access to at least one consistent, supportive individual can greatly enhance educational motivation and achievement, and mitigate the consequences of change and loss. Decisions which require children to move from one place to another should identify with the child who are the key people for providing continuity and support. The person(s) may be professional, family or friend, adult or child. Every effort should be made to sustain the contact and the relationship. It is also important to encourage endeavours by children in spheres which are important to them or for which they may show aptitude. This can provide opportunities for success and self-confidence for children who often feel that there is little positive in their lives as their family circumstances have 'failed' and they may be underachieving at school too.

Having examined the specific evidence about the education of children looked after away from home, brief consideration will now be given to the context of wider social and policy developments. These provide obstacles, challenges and also opportunities for the hitherto piece-meal and localised initiatives to have a more extensive impact.

The wider context
An issue for the 1990s?
An interesting starting point from which to begin to identify key themes may be to consider why this issue has come to the fore during the last decade, while the problem itself has existed for some time. While the contributions of individuals such as Sonia Jackson were undoubtedly crucial in highlighting this 'scandal', aspects of the current social, political and professional climate will have shaped how their message has been 'heard' and acted upon (or not). It might also be that those factors which helped draw attention to the education of children in care may also have a bearing on how the issue is addressed. In a similar vein, it has been argued that the development of the British child protection system has reflected the process through which the abuse of children was recognised and defined as a social problem during the 1970s and 1980s (Parton 1985, 1991).

Specific changes in professional perspectives have been addressed in previous chapters and chapter two provides a detailed analysis of the policy context and key ideologies which underpin current practice. What emerges is that, though there are many aspects of the current climate which provide an impetus to provide a better educational deal for young people looked after, other dimensions may potentially have the opposite effect. There is thus cause for optimism but not complacency.

New attitudes towards children

The fact that much of the evidence of unsatisfactory educational experiences was based on the accounts of care-leavers reflects a willingness to listen to young people and see them as competent commentators on their own experience. Increasingly, researchers recognise the need to engage with children in order to understand aspects of their lives (Hill 1995). This is in sharp contrast to traditional approaches which have sought to understand children by treating them as objects of study. During the 1980s sociologists developed a new approach to the study of children (Qvortrup *et al* 1994; Jenks 1996; James & Prout 1997). Asserting that childhood should be valued and understood from a child's perspective, the new sociology of childhood was critical of developmental approaches which based understanding of children on adult observation and viewed childhood simply as preparation for (more important) adult life, rather than a different (but equally valuable) stage of life. In short, this perspective views children as competent actors whose perspective on matters which affect them is valuable. The task for adults is to seek to understand this perspective.

Notions of children's rights have also changed our thinking about children. Public knowledge of the UN Convention may be limited, but well-publicised accounts of children 'divorcing' or suing their parents have created awareness that children are now entitled, in certain circumstances, to act independently of their parents and challenge their actions (Borland *et al* 1998). In chapter two we looked at the incorporation of children's rights into current policy and considered some of the associated tensions. Though the rights enshrined in policy may not always be meaningful, for example when sufficient or suitable resources are not available, children in public care are generally thought to be increasingly aware of their rights and how to exercise them. Their entitlement to education is fundamental.

In many respects therefore, changes in attitudes towards children provide a clear impetus for improving the education for children in care, but there is a flip side which could mitigate against progress. A rights discourse highlights that adults' actions in respect of children may serve their own rather than children's interests, thus challenging the widely-held view that most steps to control or influence children are for their own good (Goldson 1997). While few parents would deny that children have a right to be protected, to be cared for in a way which allows them to develop and to have their views taken into account in matters which affect them, many are uncomfortable with the concept of 'rights', preferring to think in terms of needs which, in most instances, will be met by benign adults (Borland *et al* 1998). There is mistrust that children will abuse rights, that parents and other adults will no longer be able to ensure their well-being and even that they may pose a threat to civilised society (Scraton 1997; Davis & Bourhill 1997).

These fears are reflected in public concerns about child crime and teachers' worries about indiscipline in schools (Haydon 1997). There are fears that children are out of control and that less, rather than more, tolerance is needed. The introduction of secure training centres and local police initiatives requiring children to be home by a certain time at night might be seen as indicators of this less liberal attitude. It has been argued that such expensive control measures reduce the funds available to support young people in school and so further decrease their life chances (Sparks 1998). There is also a risk that schools will respond to this less tolerant climate, which would no doubt have an adverse effect on some of the more difficult young people looked after.

Consumerism and accountability

Children's views are sought nowadays not only because they provide a child's perspective but because they are consumers of the service. Several measures introduced since the 1980s have given more power to people who use public services. In the education field, parents were given more scope to choose their children's school and schools were obliged to publish information on which they could base that choice. Within social work, open access to files and complaints procedures were introduced, while groups such as Who Cares? were formed to represent the views of children in care. In that they encourage teachers and social workers to pay more attention to the outcome of their practice and how it is received, these developments are conducive to providing a better service for looked after children.

However this trend also has the potential to disadvantage children in care. Within education, it is parents who are seen as consumers, so that children who cannot rely on that kind of personal advocacy may miss out. There is also the risk that in responding to the wishes of the majority of parents, schools will devote less time and resources to the special needs of individual children and be less willing to persevere with those who are troublesome (Blyth & Milner 1997). Despite the empowerment of consumers, children looked after remain an essentially powerless group.

Inclusion

Across the social-care spectrum, the aim since the 1970s has been to cater for people with special care or educational needs within the community rather than placing them in separate institutions or specialist provision. As a result, mainstream, community-based services are expected to find ways of catering for a range of individual needs. It is in this spirit that schools are being asked to find out and respond to the educational needs of individual children who are looked after and to accommodate the additional demands they may make. Where educational support services have been developed to further this aim, their input has been very much welcomed by school and social work staff alike (Fletcher-Campbell 1997).

For the majority of children looked after, the principle of inclusion must be a bonus. An environment which expects diversity and seeks to individualise support is to be welcomed. However we noted in chapter six that a significant minority of young people who find themselves in care have substantial educational difficulties and that delaying access to specialist help may compound their difficulties (HMI 1990; Triseliotis *et al* 1995; SWSI 1996). In addition, requiring over-stretched services to accommodate the most demanding children, without support, may have an adverse effect on the wider school.

Partnership

'Partnership' is undoubtedly a key concept of the 1980s and 1990s. Children's legislation governing each part of the United Kingdom now requires that both parents share responsibility for bringing up their children, even when they no longer live together. Local authority social work departments are asked to work in partnership with parents and to collaborate with other professionals within and outwith their authority. Indeed, as parents now share responsibility for their own children, so local authority departments have a shared responsibility (with parents) for children who are looked after.

Despite a number of difficulties in interpreting what 'partnership' means in practice (Tisdall 1997), the ascendancy of the 'partnership' notion has undoubtedly contributed to a climate conducive to tackling the shared issue of education for children in care. Indeed it may be thought that, having instituted corporate responsibility and collaborative processes, for example the preparation of children's services plans, effective collaboration will necessarily follow. However Blyth and Milner (1997) refute this optimism strongly, pointing to several counter pressures towards continued fragmentation.

Commenting on the English system, Blyth and Milner suggest that present arrangements for inter-agency cooperation are unlikely to overcome schools' unwillingness to take pupils with special educational needs, especially when these requests are not backed by effective parents. There are also indications that financial stringency poses a barrier to effective cooperation since each department closely guards its own budget (Kendrick *et al* 1996). Similarly, among front-line staff there is also the risk that job insecurity and low morale encourages a siege mentality rather than proactive cooperation among teachers and social workers.

The experience of the Equal Chances project, reported in the previous chapter (Fletcher 1998) confirms that the existence of collaborative structures and general commitment to partnership principles will not, in themselves, produce a better deal for children looked after away from home. Rather, specific proactive systems and practices need to be developed, established and monitored. As Blyth and Milner conclude: 'Put simply, the local authority, acting as corporate parent, needs to take its responsibilities more seriously'.

In essence, we are arguing that, while changes in attitudes towards children, increasing demands for professional accountability and notions of working in partnership have helped create a climate in which the education of children looked after is receiving more attention, aspects of these developments may also act against the interests of children in public care. Alternatively, there is the danger that, without proper monitoring, formal mechanisms and commitment to principles give the illusion that progress is being made, without significantly changing the experience of children and young people.

Priority to education and social exclusion

Current policy initiatives perhaps provide most cause for optimism that improving educational opportunities will remain a priority, attracting increasing attention and resources. Improving all children's educational attainment is a priority for the present government and is identified as one of the key elements in the government's programme to reduce social exclusion. Indeed the three themes identified in a recent consultation paper on this initiative (Scottish Office 1998c) would apply equally to programmes for the education of children in care:

- the need for increased **co-ordination** of effort
- the need to identify interventions which can **prevent** social exclusion
- the need to develop (or expand) **innovative** approaches to the problem.

Conditions for making progress would seem to be broadly favourable, though several important obstacles remain.

Missing from the research literature...

While there is a broad consensus about the type of basic structures and practices required, detailed knowledge to inform more sophisticated planning and targeting of services is not available. We need more understanding of how different groups of young people are affected, how children's education/care experience develops over time and of the factors which influence this process. Further, the focus of existing research has been largely on professional perspectives. Understanding of the detailed views of children and young people themselves and of their parents remains limited as information has, in the main, been gained from wider surveys rather than specific care/education research. Several relevant innovative projects have been identified, but rarely evaluated systematically. As noted earlier, virtually all of the research was carried out in England and we lack evidence of how the findings might apply to practice in Scotland.

Differentiation

Most studies still talk as though children in care were a homogeneous group. A notable exception was the Aldgate, Heath and Colton study which focused on children in foster care. In so doing, this important study challenged some long-held assumptions, for example about the expectations of teachers, and that it was enough to provide a stable caring placement. We need more differentiated studies of specific groups of children, taking account of differences in ages, characteristics, types of placement and educational settings. Most information is available about secondary school children in long-term care. The situation of primary school children is less well known. Pre-school education appears not to have been considered at all, yet considerable numbers of children under five are placed away from home, often on an emergency or short-term basis. It would also be helpful to examine the circumstances of younger children who enter care with reasonable attainments to understand what processes help sustain good progress.

The few studies which have considered academic work have focused on traditional subject areas, with little attention to personal and social education, or to sport, art, music and so on. The implications of gender and ethnic background have hardly been considered, though there is clear evidence that boys' and girls' general school experience is quite different (Howe 1997). There is a general lack of information about the education of children with disabilities who are looked after. Children in special education appear to be well supported emotionally but their curriculum is often restricted and they are not necessarily fulfilling their potential. Parents can be powerful advocates for children with disabilities. Are looked after children missing out?

Locational differences have not been explored. For example, little is known about the situation of children in rural areas or of those who are placed in areas which contrast markedly with their own backgrounds.

Longitudinal research

Much of the research has been of the snap-shot kind. Longitudinal research has generally concerned care careers, with educational changes an incidental consideration. It would be valuable to understand how care and education careers interact, with particular attention to key decision and change points; corresponding systems of assessment and review (for example, for those with special educational needs); and the inter-agency and interprofessional communication processes involved.

Discontinuity is a major issue. The existing research shows this is a complex matter: placement moves can necessitate school transfer and school issues can lead to placement moves. While the disadvantages of many moves are clear, some children have managed to cope. What factors allow unavoidable discontinuity to be managed? When children experience multiple changes at once or over time, is stress reduced if these can be phased or partialised? Children have rights to be consulted, if they have sufficient understanding. How can children be helped to make sense of, and make the best of, the decisions and changes which affect them?

Understanding processes from children's perspectives

One factor seldom mentioned in the research but raised by Fletcher of the Who Cares? Trust is the help children receive, or do not receive, to handle the pain and turmoil in their lives, including the shame of not having been able to learn. Interestingly, SWSI inspectors recommended that some of the pupils in secure care needed counselling related to this in order to be able to start learning (SWSI 1996). This offers a different perception of the school/ care divide and requires joint responsibilities to promote children's learning.

Both education and care experiences tend to be conceptualised largely in terms of a child's interaction with adults (teachers, carers, social workers, parents). Yet other children can be crucial for children's educational, social and emotional development – with potentially positive or negative effects. Little is known about how friendships (and their disruption) affect children's management of educational and placement changes. School-mates can be important confidants and supporters, while foster carers' children and fellow residents may facilitate, or interfere with, commitment to school and schooling.

Bullying in school or within the core setting can be a significant block to learning and/or attendance. We need more understanding of children's experience to help ensure that support mechanisms are effective.

Understanding inter-professional processes

The barriers to joint working in terms of differing professional roles, responsibilities, ideologies and perspectives are well recognised. Although these continue to be important, our understanding of traditional differences may be out of date. Developments in teaching encourage supporting the whole child, while social workers are required to be more task-focused and address education as a priority. We saw from the literature that supporting the education of children in care raises dilemmas on both sides. For example, teachers who want to be caring must beware of being intrusive and care-staff who are mindful of children's right to make choices are expected to be firm in ensuring reluctant children attend school. Examination of attitudes within and across the two professions would promote understanding and inform staff development and training. Existing accounts have relied mainly on interviews, sometimes of one group only. It would be helpful to supplement this by extending some of the observational and vignette techniques which have been developed to study interprofessional relationships in other areas.

Project evaluation

Several examples have been described of apparently successful teaching support through link workers. Few of these schemes have been evaluated systematically. This is important if resources are to be used most effectively. The Manchester Teaching Service is recognised as a model of effective inter-agency working and teaching support to children in care. However a report by the National Children's Bureau, while recognising the valuable work of the service, suggested a change in its role which would involve more consultancy to social work staff and carers (Rea-Price & Pugh 1996). Changes such as these should, in part, be based on evidence about what does, or does not, help children.

Concluding remarks

While further research is needed, it is equally important to try and ensure that the lessons of previous work have been applied. Certainly, there is evidence of some shift in orientation by teachers and social workers to bridge the education/care gulf, whilst formal policy and structures are conducive to more cooperation. What remains to be done is to ensure that both routine communication and key decision-making meetings respond to the educational implications of plans for a child. Conversely, attention is needed to how actions and moves at school affect a child's home circumstances. Managing change, loss and unfamiliarity in the two major spheres of a child's life is a difficult process. In addition to focusing on learning in school, priority must be given to maximising continuity and support for children and young people during such changes.

Appendix: Summaries of Key Studies

Aldgate, J., Heath, A. & Colton, M. (1993) *The Educational Progress of Children in Foster Care*

This study was supported by the ESRC and undertaken as part of phase 2 of their Children in Care Research Programme. Its overall aim was to identify factors contributing to the attainment of children in long term foster care. The sample was 49 foster children (26 boys, 23 girls) aged 8–14. All were in mainstream state schools in one English county and had been in care for a minimum of six months. Many had been in their placements for several years, the mean and median length being six years. Thus this was a sample of children in fairly stable circumstances, living in the optimum form of care available. The children were predominantly white.

The research design was partly cross-sectional and partly longitudinal. Attainment and behaviour were measured at the start and at yearly intervals over the next two years. Their scores were compared with a control group of 58 children living in circumstances similar to those in the children's birth family. Each child's individual progress over the two years was also measured. Several instruments were used, including three standardised measures of attainment which were administered three times, at yearly intervals: Suffolk Reading Test (or NFER's EH1 for children over 14 years); NFER's British Picture Vocabulary Scale; NFER Basic Mathematics test; Rutter's two parallel questionnaires for parents and teachers to assess children's behaviour (at the start and end of the study); Personal interviews with carers/ parents, social workers and children

Key Findings:

- Children in foster care and the control group were performing well below the national average but there was no statistically significant difference between the groups. Despite being in favourable placements, there was little evidence of foster children catching up while they were in care.

- There was no evident relationship between changes in legal status or placement and educational attainment. It might have been expected that children in the most settled and secure placements would perform better but this was not confirmed. However educational progress was higher where there was an expectation of future stability, whether on the basis of fostering or adoption.

- On all three tests and in all rounds of testing the children who came into care for suspected child abuse or neglect scored significantly lower than did the other foster children. Although there was some evidence of progress in reading, the educational disadvantage of early abuse and neglect had not been overcome, even if children were in long-term settled placements.

- Teachers set expectations of children's future attainment at a lower level than did carers, social workers or the children themselves. Over time the test scores did not support the view that teachers' low expectations were self-filling prophesies. Rather they reflected an accurate assessment of children's ability. Social workers were unduly optimistic.

- Reading scores did improve among children (in foster care and control group) who received special help with reading.

- Children in foster homes where at least one carer was educated to 'A' level did better on the reading and vocabulary tests than other foster children but did not make greater progress over time. Children placed with these highly qualified carers seemed to have made progress before the study began, suggesting that early educational intervention may be necessary to secure an 'escape from disadvantage'.

- Foster carers provided a more educationally stimulating environment than the control parents. They attended school events, discussed children's progress with teachers, helped with homework, encouraged them to borrow books from the library and took them on educational leisure activities. Despite this the foster children did little better than the control group.

- Progress was unrelated to the amount of contact with the birth parents.

- Even when there was no evidence of behaviour or emotional problems, foster children scored below the national average in reading, vocabulary and maths. This was not the case for children in the comparison group among whom children with no behavioural or emotional problems reached national average levels of attainment.

- Although they discussed education on visits to foster homes, 'attending to children's educational attainment' and 'helping children develop special talents' were accorded a low priority. Social workers' top concerns were to 'help children make successful attachments'.

- Social workers considered that child care reviews were the forum in which educational progress should be monitored and 82% said they would expect a teacher to be present. Carers and social workers' views were divergent on who should take educational decisions.

Different aspects of the study are reported in the following articles:

Aldgate, J. (1990) Foster Children at school: success or failure? The 1990 Hilda Lewis Memorial Lecture. *Adoption and Fostering*, 14 (4).

Aldgate, J., Heath, A. & Colton, M. (1992) Educational Attainment and Stability in Long-term Foster Care. *Children & Society* , 6 (2): 91–103.

Aldgate, J., Heath, A., Colton, M. & Sim, M. (1993) Social Work and the education of children in foster care. *Adoption and Fostering* , 17 (3).

Heath, A., Colton, M. & Aldgate, J. (1994) Failure to Escape: A Longitudinal Study of Foster Children's Educational Attainment. *British Journal of Social Work,* 24: 241–260.

Colton, M. & Heath, A. (1994) Attainment and Behaviour of Children in Care and at Home. *Oxford Review of Education,* 20 (3).

Colton, M., Heath, A. & Aldgate, J. (1995) Factors which influence the Educational Attainment of Children in Foster Care. *Community Alternatives,* 7 (1).

Berridge, D., Brodie, I., Ayre, P., Barrett, D., Henderson, B. & Wenman, H. (1996) *Hello – Is Anyone Listening? The Education of Young People in Residential Care.*

This report was based on the second stage of a three-year collaborative research programme between Northborough Social Services (to preserve anonymity, the names of local authority and residential homes were altered) and the University of Luton. The focus of Stage 1 was to examine the perceived impact of the substantial reorganisation and other changes to residential child-care services in Northborough in 1993–1994. For this second part of the study attention was limited to examining the educational experiences of young people living in children's homes through:

- exploring the perspectives of the senior managers in education and social services on current issues and problems in providing schooling to young people accommodated in Northborough's children's homes

- investigating similar issues in association with staff in certain residential homes in Northborough and representatives of schools or units catering for their residents

- gathering basic statistical information on the current educational situation and status of residents in selected children's homes, together with young people's perspectives on education

- investigating the educational environment of certain children's homes and the way in which schooling matters were approached.

The sample consisted of three of five existing residential homes in the area. Thirteen young people were living in the homes at the time of research (October 1995), seven male and six female. All were described as white and most were aged between 12 and 15. Interviews were held with selected managers in social services and education and with a representative from the social services education support team. Researchers visited the three homes as observer participants over a period of three days. During this time interviews were held with heads of homes and a cross-section of staff. In association with heads of homes/ keyworkers, specific background information was gathered on young people and their educational status. They also participated generally in the life of the home during this period, eating meals etc. Visits took place to a small number of Northborough schools attended by current or ex-residents. An interview was held with a school representative to explore their perceptions of providing education to young people looked after in residential accommodation. Interviews took place with groups or individual young people from the homes.

Key findings (shown according to the main research subjects):
Managers
- An awareness from social services and education managers that education is important in the lives of looked after children but a general feeling that social services gave insufficient priority to educational issues both in planning and in relation to individual children. This reflected an overall perception of low expectation of academic achievement for looked after children from social service staff.
- A feeling that most schools were sensitive to the needs of children in residential care. Additionally, school exclusion was less of a problem in Northborough than many other authorities.
- A general view that recent government education reforms had a negative effect on the education of looked after children.

Young people
- A higher proportion of Northborough residents were attending schools than is apparent in the author's national research in three local authorities.
- At some stage, all young people had changed schools for reasons other than age, although most had occurred before entry to the residential unit.
- Care plans did not exist for most of the young people. Of the four that existed, only one referred to educational issues.
- The majority of young people interviewed cited emotional and family problems as being the main reasons for difficulties in attendance and concentration at school, aggravated by the attitudes of fellow pupils and teachers towards themselves. Problems stemming from the care process itself or the residential units specifically were felt to be less salient.
- A majority of interviewees considered education to be important for future employment. Furthermore, young people who had 'failed' in the school system were now being encouraged and were motivated to undertake further study post–16.

Schools
- Interviewees did not see young people looked after in residential care as a discrete group or one which was inevitably problematic. In turn, although emotional problems experienced by the children affected behaviour and academic achievement, many children did not experience such problems; thus interviewees stressed the need to treat children as individuals.
- Relationships between schools and social workers were positive. In particular, it was felt that social workers now took greater account of

education in planning for young people. However, more feedback from social workers would have been appreciated.

- Much poorer relationships were reported to exist between schools and children's homes. Residential staff were also said to have had very limited involvement in schools. Interviewees were on the whole unaware of staff attending parent's evenings and other school functions such as sports days.

The Educational Environment of Children's Homes

- The physical environment and resources of the homes seemed to offer young people generally adequate support, though a lack of appropriate reading material in general and reference books in particular was noted.
- Staff were generally very keen to promote attendance at school and college but there was sometimes less focus on their attainment, some staff seeming resigned to very poor levels of academic achievement. Workers were, on the whole, willing to offer support but tended to take a lead from the young people rather than initiating action.
- There was not observed to be a culture of informal learning, for example the television and an impressive programme of outings and holidays seemed to offer many opportunities but had generally not been taken up.
- Most staff were strongly committed to avoiding actively a culture of non-attendance but a significant minority seemed to adopt a somewhat passive approach.
- Whilst a marked commitment in principle to the completion of homework was observed, this was not always supported by a standard 'homework routine' or by a knowledge of the school's expectations of each young person, sometimes making the principle difficult to put into practice.
- Standards of principles and practice for the daily routine of young people not attending school were better developed in some homes than in others.

Heads of Homes and Staff

- There was concern in the three units visited about levels of staff sickness and dependency on agency staff.
- Residential staff felt that they were offering encouragement and support regarding education that had often previously been absent in their families. However, practices varied among the three homes.
- Liaison and communication between residential homes and schools was generally considered to be inadequate. Furthermore, care planning was felt to be unsatisfactory. It was unsurprising, therefore, that educational planning did not receive higher priority.
- Staff expectations of residents' educational achievements were low and were generally restricted solely to attendance.
- Staff stated that, whenever appropriate, they attended parents' evenings and other school functions. This contradicts what was said by the teachers.

- Staff were unclear what their approach should be when young people were absent from school and in the units during the day. They were also unsure about what measures could legitimately be taken to get children out of bed in the morning and off to school. However, there was a desire for training for better understanding of education issues and processes.

Fletcher-Campbell, F. & Hall, C. (1990) *Changing Schools? Changing People?*

This NFER/ESRC funded research aimed at reviewing the arrangements for the education of children in care. Following on from issues raised by Jackson and others, the study examined concerns centring on the poor educational experiences of children in care, with specific focus on the lack of a coordinated approach by social services, education departments and other agencies. The research had two phases. The first was a questionnaire survey of all social services departments in England and Wales. The second included both qualitative and quantitative work. Semi-structured interviews were conducted with field and residential care managers and social workers, staff in education units attached to residential homes, education department officers, educational psychologists, education welfare officers/ social workers, foster carers and young people in care. In addition, through a questionnaire survey, data was obtained on 402 children of statutory school age who had been in care for at least six months. This covered: background details – age, gender, ethnicity; care careers – reasons for reception into care, length of time in care and/or care episodes, placements in care; education careers – schools attended, school-related problems, anticipated levels of achievement and educational qualifications; the distribution of responsibility for educational issues between social workers and carers.

Key findings:

- Responses indicated that very few local authorities were able to supply information about where children in care were educated. Indeed, there was no way of quickly determining on a national, or even local scale, the numbers in special schools, alternative units, suspended or excluded, or in mainstream education. On the whole, this indicated a need to adjust the way information on individual education careers of looked after children is mapped. Data was mainly contained in case files with no separate section on education and no means of extracting or aggregating information to highlight problems or specific needs.

- Though school continuity was generally considered desirable, practical difficulties were often overriding. Therefore, it was suggested that the benefits of a school close to the new home and the availability of friends in the locality sometimes outweighed the disadvantage of remaining at the previous school.

- Foster carers often held the responsibility of finding a new school as social workers generally considered them to be best placed to negotiate with schools. However, where they encountered difficulties, it was not immediately clear that support was forthcoming and some carers admitted feeling left to get on with it. The authors also suggest that social workers evaluated schools purely on their social aspects, ignoring academic progress and attainment.

- Many looked after children resented the presence of teachers at care reviews where their domestic situation was discussed. Some social services overcame this by admitting teachers only to part of the review where educational matters were considered; others used written reports; others overrode children's wishes if they thought that it would be useful to have the teacher present throughout.

- In terms of joint working, there were various opportunities for professionals to meet together. However, although pockets of effective practice emerged from this, there was ample evidence of rigid professional boundaries. Whilst good cooperation may have existed at one level, it did not necessarily apply elsewhere.

- A clear interrelationship between care and education issues emerged. Suspension or exclusion from school caused problems for residential homes who in turn found it difficult to negotiate with schools on future options for the young people concerned. Similarly, continuation of foster placements was sometimes dependent on the child attending school since tensions were heightened if they were around the house all day.

Fletcher-Campbell, F. (1997) *The Education of Children who are Looked After*

This follow-up to the 1990 study indicated that the importance of children's education while looked after was more widely recognised but that action to improve the situation remained patchy. The specific aims of the research were to: identify changes in policy, procedures and practice resulting from the DfE Circular; explore the implications of these changes at local authority and school level; describe the perceived effects on young people's educational experiences careers and attainment; establish criteria for good practice within a context in which the interaction of social and educational needs is critical.

The research was carried out in two stages. First, a questionnaire was sent to all local authorities in England and Wales, requesting information about their present and planned provision for the education of children looked after away from home. Exploratory interviews were also carried out in 14 local authorities known to have specialist provision. The second stage involved case studies in six authorities identified as having a fairly well-established discrete education support service for children looked after. Interviews were held with key people including carers, teachers, specialist staff and young people. In addition relevant documentation was examined and meetings attended.

Key Findings:

The Survey of Local Authorities

- Less than half (28) of the 66 local education authorities which completed the questionnaire had an LEA officer with identified responsibility for the education of looked after children.

- Few schools had a named person responsible for looked-after pupils.

- 25 authorities had a written policy regarding the education of children looked after, usually drawn up jointly between education and social services. The nature of documentation varied widely, from broad statements of intent or principles to more focused action plans.

- 26 authorities had discrete teaching posts for looked-after children, mostly jointly resourced and managed by education and social services.

- A wide range of managerial and organisational problems were encountered in supporting the education of looked after children. These were mainly attributed to inflexible professional boundaries, lack of experience in inter-professional collaboration and poor information management. A few authorities had developed initiatives to overcome these problems.

- Few authorities kept central records of data on the educational placement or progress of children looked after. Only a few authorities had carried out any monitoring or evaluation of the service.

- 51 authorities said they had plans to develop services to support the education of children looked-after.

Education Support Services

- Arrangements for funding varied across authorities and the nature of services reflected local circumstances and need.

- Having established a discrete education support service, policies, procedures and documentation had undergone rapid evolution.

- The separate services perceived themselves as mediators between education and social services departments. The ability to move with ease between social work and education were key skills for staff in specialist support services.

- Specialist staff were keen to assist schools and carers in supporting young people who were looked after and did not offer long-term direct support to any individual young person. They engaged in formal training of colleagues across agencies and engaged in a range of supportive initiatives such as homework clubs.

- Most services focused on adolescents, though referrals of primary school age children were increasing.

- The accessibility and responsiveness of the services was much appreciated by carers and teachers.

Carers
- All carers were convinced of the importance of education and prepared to take action in support of young people (the carers in the research had been identified as particularly skilled and experienced at promoting education).
- Foster carers promoting education included those with widely different levels of experience in the education system.
- Carers were generally keen to work in partnership with other professionals.
- Within residential units the leadership of the unit manager was influential but sometimes educational support teams could enhance young people's education in units without effective leadership.
- Not having a school placement adversely affected placements, sometimes resulting in breakdown.
- Residential staff agreed units were far more difficult to manage when young people were not at school during the day.
- Some residential units had a written policy which clearly stated the aims and practice of the unit in relation to education.

Schools
- Schools differed considerably in their attitude towards pupils who were looked after. Some were welcoming and supportive, others were wary and anticipated problems.
- It was often difficult to arrange admission to a new school for a child who was looked after.
- Difficulties in arranging admissions were eased when the school and other professionals worked together to develop a strategy in advance.
- There was some evidence that some schools more readily excluded looked-after pupils, believing that carers would be available to care for them. However other schools only excluded young people after serious incidents and managed their return sensitively, working in partnership with carers and the education support service.
- To prevent exclusion, the school placements of many looked after children required maintenance, regular monitoring and effective communication.
- There was evidence of considerable success with some very difficult young people where schools were prepared to support and encourage them and work in partnership with other agencies.

Francis, J., Thomson, G.O.B. & Mills, S. (1995) *The Quality of the Educational Experience of Children in Care,* **University of Edinburgh**

This study examined the educational experiences of 27 primary and secondary pupils in the care of Lothian Region. Fourteen pupils had been admitted to care in 1992, remaining for at least two years, and 13 had first come into care in 1994, at least six weeks before the study was carried out. The first group are referred to as 'retrospective' and the second as 'prospective'. The research was based largely on a study of school and social work records, though in relation to the prospective group, social workers, carers and teachers completed questionnaires about school attendance, performance and behaviour. In addition, some of the children and young people were interviewed.

Summary of findings
Referral and admission to care
At the time of initial referral to the social work department, school problems were indicated in five of the fourteen pupils in the *retrospective group*. This had increased to twelve on admission to care. Three were excluded from school and a further three had been excluded previously for a temporary period. School difficulties are recorded as contributing to the decision to admit to care in eight cases. Seven pupils came into care on an emergency basis and ten were the subject of compulsory measures. In the *prospective group*, school problems were noted in social work records for only one pupil at referral and for three on admission, one young person having been excluded. However school records indicated behaviour difficulties in relation to eight pupils. Problem behaviour included disruptive sexualised behaviour and the physical and verbal abuse of staff and pupils. There had been four temporary exclusions. Ten of this group had been admitted as emergencies, six on a compulsory basis.

School and placement changes
In the two years since the *retrospective* group had been admitted to care there were frequent changes of school. Eight had more than four moves, four moved two or three times and two made the natural transition from primary to secondary. Many of these moves were described as meeting educational needs. While there was remarkable stability in the care placements of the six primary-aged children, the older ones did not fare so well. Only one teenage boy remained in his original placement. Four other boys had two or three moves and two girls moved six or seven times. Among the *prospective* group, eight of the thirteen had changes in care placement, five being teenagers who experienced two or more moves. Change of school occurred on four occasions

Reviews
With the *retrospective group*, the education of all 14 pupils was discussed at the 72 hour review, though an educational representative was present at only one. Attendance improved at the 85 on-going reviews with educational staff present at 26. However half of the pupils had no representative from the education department at any of their reviews. Representation was more likely for those in residential care than in foster care. With the *prospective group*, education was discussed at nine out of thirteen 72 hour reviews and education staff were present at three. At the 22 subsequent reviews, educational matters were noted in all cases and five were attended by a representative from

education. However, for nearly three quarters of the pupils, no-one from the education department attended any review.

Educational progress
Incomplete records of the *retrospective* group meant that the authors had difficulty in evaluation: 'all that can be said on the basis of the minimum information available is that these pupils were performing at a uniformly modest to poor level'. Data for the *prospective* sample was more accessible and demonstrated that the primary group fared better than the secondary. The authors suggest that, 'the earlier educational intervention and support occurs, the better'. Teachers were more positive about the future of the primary group than the secondary group in relation to attendance and behaviour as well as attainment. In this there was a divergence in the views of teachers and social workers, with the former perceiving pupils as below average and the latter, including carers, taking a more optimistic view.

The views of the children and young people
The two primary children said they would like more time to talk over their school problems with someone. Four of the five teenagers said they could cope better at school before they came into care. Care was seen as providing emotional stability. Like the younger children, there was a recognition of the need to have someone to talk to who was interested in them.

Jackson, S.
Jackson's work has been highly influential in drawing attention to the poor educational experience of children in care. She is critical of social workers, carers and teachers for stereo-typing children in care as low achievers and advocates making residential and foster homes educationally rich environments. She argues powerfully that education is the main route out of disadvantage and should consequently be a high priority for children in care.

Key studies:
(1) Residential Care and Education
Case study of a children's home which made a determined effort to put education at the top of its agenda. The strategy included work on: staff training, attitudes and expectations; how children saw themselves and were viewed by others; relationships with schools, teachers and other professionals; direct measures to improve the children's school performance; attempts to create an educational ambience in the home.

A significant element was the appointment of an educational liaison officer. A teacher by training, her main role was to act as an intermediary between care staff, children and teachers. This included attention to routine communication and defusing conflicts at an early stage. Schools stopped suspending children, though this had previously occurred almost weekly. Within the home, a greater emphasis was placed on completing homework, an hour being set aside each evening during which two teachers were available to help any child in difficulty. In addition, the link teacher arranged home tutoring and recruited outside volunteers to help with homework. Jackson reported that being able to hand in acceptable pieces of work transformed children's attitudes towards going to school and changed teachers' perceptions of their ability and potential. Education in the broadest sense was 'woven into the fabric of daily life' as children were encouraged to participate in local clubs, take up hobbies and become well-informed about the world and current affairs.

Jackson, S. (1987) Residential care and education, *Children and Society*, 4: 335–350.

(2) Successful in Care is a retrospective study of 152 people who had been in care as children and had obtained 5 GCSE or 'O' level passes at grade C or above or had entered further or higher education. The research aimed to identify the process by which some children are able to succeed in education, despite being brought up in care.

Key findings:
- The care experiences of the high achievers were similar to those of other young people in care ie characterised by many moves, disruption and insecurity.
- The most consistent response was that they felt unsupported by social workers, care staff and teachers. Their ability had not been recognised or their achievement valued by social work staff and at school they experienced discrimination by teachers and bullying by peers.
- For some, foster carers had provided important encouragement and acted as advocates with schools and social services.
- Natural parents had also been important in helping sustain motivation.
- All the men and over 90% of the women interviewed had gone on to some form of further education after leaving school. Compared with other care leavers, more were in employment, fewer women were single parents and only one person was homeless. The group's post-care experience thus confirmed the link between educational attainment and 'escape from disadvantage'.

Reported in Jackson, S. (1994) Education in Residential and Foster Care, *Oxford Review of Education*, 20 (3): 267–279.

Other key publications:
Jackson, S. (1987) *The Education of Children in Care*. Bristol Papers in Applied Social Studies. University of Bristol.
Jackson, S. (1989) Education of Children in Care. In: Kahan, B. (ed) *Child Care Research, Policy and Practice*. Hodder & Stoughton.
Jackson, S. (1995) 'Transforming Lives: The Crucial Role of Education for Young People in the Care System'. First Tory Laughland Memorial Lecture. Who Cares? Trust.

Bibliography

Adler, M., Petch, A. & Tweedie, J. (1989) *Parental Choice and Educational Policy.* Edinburgh University Press.

Aldgate, J. (1990) 'Foster Children at School: Success or Failure? The 1990 Hilda Lewis Memorial Lecture'. *Adoption and Fostering* ,14(4).

Aldgate, J., Heath, A., Colton, M. & Simm, M. (1993) 'Social Work and Education in Foster Care'. *Adoption & Fostering*, 17(3): 25–34.

Aldagte, J., Mallucio, A., & Reeves, C. (1989) *Adolescents in Foster Families.* Batsford.

Aldgate, J. & Tunstill, J. (1995) *Making Sense of Section 17: Implementing Services for Children in Need within the 1989 Children Act.* HMSO.

Antonovsky, A. (1985) *Health Stress and Coping.* San Francisco: Jossey-Bass.

Antonovsky, A. (1987) *Unravelling the Mystery of Health.* San Francisco: Jossey-Bass.

Armstrong, D.K., Galloway, D. & Tomlinson, S. (1993) 'Assessing Special Educational Needs: The Child's Contribution'. *British Educational Research Journal*, 19(2): 121–131.

Audit Commission (1994) *Seen But Not Heard: Co-ordinating Child Health and Social Services for Children in Need.* HMSO.

Bald, J., Bean, J., Meegan, F. (1995) *A Book of My Own.* Who Cares? Trust.

Banks, M., Bates, I., Breakwell, G., Brynner, J., Emler, N., Jamieson, L. & Roberts, K. (1992) *Careers and Identities.* Milton Keynes: Open University Press.

Barr, J. (1994) 'Policy Frameworks and Policy Planning'. In: Munn, P. (ed) *Schooling with Care.* Edinburgh: Scottish Office.

Beardslee, W.R. (1989) 'The Role of Self-Understanding in Resilient Individuals: The Development of a Perspective'. *American Journal of Orthopsychiatry*, 59(2): 266–278.

Bebbington, A.R. & Miles, J. (1989) 'The Background of Children Who Enter Local Authority Care'. *British Journal of Social Work*, 19: 349–368.

Berridge, D. (1985) *Children's Homes.* Oxford: Blackwell.

Berridge, D. & Brodie, I. (1996) 'Disparate or Desperate? Residential Care in England'. Paper presented to the International Conference on Residential Child Care, Glasgow.

Berridge, D. & Brodie, I. (1998) *Children's Homes Revisited.* London: Jessica Kingsley Publishers.

Berridge, D., Brodie, I., Ayre, P., Barrett, D., Henderson, B. & Wenman, H. (1996) *Hello – is Anybody Listening? The Education of Young People in Residential Care.* University of Luton.

Berridge, D. & Cleaver, H. (1997) *Foster Home Breakdown.* Oxford: Basic Blackwell.

Biehal, N., Clayden, J., Stein, M. & Wade, J. (1992) *Prepared for Living?* National Children's Bureau.

Biehal, N., Clayden, J., Stein, M. & Wade, J. (1995) *Moving On: Young people and Leaving Care Schemes.* HMSO.

Blyth, E. & Milner, J. (1993) 'Exclusion from School: First Step on Exclusion from Society'. *Children & Society,* 7(3): 255–268.

Blyth, E. & Milner, J. (1994) 'Exclusion from School and Victim-blaming'. *Oxford Review of Education,* 20(3).

Blyth, E. & Milner, J. (1997) *Social Work With Children The Educational Perspective.* Longman.

Borge, A. (1996) 'Developmental Pathways of Behaviour Problems in the Young Child: Factors Associated with Continuity and Change'. *Scandinavian Journal of Psychology,* 37: 195–204.

Borland, M. (1992) 'Evaluation of Statements of Functions and Objectives of Scottish Children's Homes'. In: *The Review of Residential Child Care in Scotland: Three Supporting Research Papers.* Edinburgh: Scottish Office Central Research Unit.

Borland, M. (1996) *Review of Statements of Functions and Objectives in Residential Child Care.* Edinburgh: Social Work Services Inspectorate.

Borland, M. & Hill, M. (1996) 'Teenagers in Britain: Empowered or Embattled'. *Youth & Policy,* 55: 56–68.

Borland, M., Laybourn, A., Hill, M. & Brown, J. (1998) *Middle Childhood.* Jessica Kingsley.

Borland, M., O'Hara, G. & Triseliotis, J. (1991) 'Placement Outcomes for Children with Special Needs'. *Adoption and Fostering,* 15(2).

Broad, B. (1997) 'Lessons for Life'. *Community Care,* 13–19 February.

Brodie, I. & Berridge, D. (1996) *School Exclusion.* University of Luton Press.

Bruce, N. (1983) 'Social Work and Education'. In: Lishman, J. (ed) *Collaboration and Conflict.* Research Highlights 7. Aberdeen University.

Bowlby, J. (1951) *Maternal Care and Mental Health.* World Health Organisation.

Buchanan, A., Wheal, A. & Coker, R. (1993) *Answering Back.* Dolphin Project. Department of Social Work Studies, University of Southampton.

Bullock, R., Little, M. & Milham, S. (1993) *Going Home.* Aldershot: Dartmouth.

Carlen, P., Gleeson, D. & Wardhaugh, J. (1992) *Truancy: The Politics of Compulsory Schooling.* Milton Keynes: Open University Press.

Central Advisory Council for Education (England) (1967) *Children and their Primary Schools.* Report by Lady Plowden. Central Advisory Council for Education (England).

Cheung, S.Y. & Heath, A. (1994) 'After Care: The Education and Occupation of Adults Who Have Been in Care'. *Oxford Review of Education,* 20(3).

Children in Scotland (ed) (1998) *Children's Rights = Human Rights?* Edinburgh: Children in Scotland.

Chisholm, W. (1998) 'Private Nurseries to Press Wilson on Safeguards'. *The Scotsman*, 28.2.98.

Cleaver, H. (1996) *Focus on Teenagers*. HMSO.

Cliffe, D. & Berridge, D. (1991) *Closing Children's Homes: An End to Residential Child Care?* National Children's Bureau.

Clyde, Lord (1992) *Report of the Inquiry into the Removal of Children from Orkney*. Edinburgh: Scottish Office.

Cochran, M., Larner, D., Riley, D., Gunnarson, L. & Henderson, C. R. (1990) *Extending Families: The Social Networks of Parents and their Children*. Cambridge University Press.

Colton, M. (1988) *Dimensions of Substitute Child Care*. Aldershot: Avebury.

Colton, M., Drury, C. & Williams, M. (1995a) 'Children in Need: Definition, Identification and Support'. *Social Work*, 25: 711–728.

Colton, M., Heath, A. & Aldgate, J. (1995b) 'Factors Which Influence the Educational Attainment of Children in Foster Family Care'. *Community Alternatives*, 7(1): 15–38.

Colton, M. & Hellinckx, W. (eds) (1993) *Child Care in the EC*. Aldershot: Ashgate.

Cooper, P. (1993) *Effective Schools for Disaffected Students*. Routledge.

Coopersmith, S. (1990) *Self-esteem Inventories*. Palo Alto: Consulting Psychologists Press.

Cullen, M.A. & Lloyd, G. (1997) *Exclusions from School and Alternatives Vol 2. Alternative Education Provision for Excluded Pupils: A Literature Review*. Edinburgh: Moray House Institute of Education, Heriot-Watt University.

Davis, H. & Bourhill, M. (1997) '"Crisis": The Demonisation of Children and Young People'. In: Scraton, P. (ed) *'Childhood' in Crisis*. UCL Press.

Dean, D. (1992) 'Moving Towards Change: The Role of People, Place and Programme in Creating a Residential Therapeutic Environment for Children'. In: Lloyd, G (ed) *Chosen with Care? Responses to Disturbing and Disruptive Behaviour*. Edinburgh: Moray House Publications.

Department for Education and Department of Health (1994) *The Education of Children being Looked after by Local Authorities*. Circular Nos 13/94 and DH LAC (94). DfE.

Department of Health (1985) *Social Work Decisions in Child Care*. DHSS.

Department of Health (1991) *Patterns and Outcomes in Child Placement*. HMSO.

Department of Health (1996) *Focus on Teenagers*. HMSO.

Downes, C. (1992) *Separation Revisited*. Aldershot: Ashgate.

Dunbar, R. (1987) 'Placement in List G Schools'. In: SED. Regional Psychological Services (ed). *Alternative Approaches to Children with Behavioural and Emotional Difficulties: Professional Development Initiatives 1986–87*.

Ennew, J. (1995) 'Outside Childhood: Street Children's Rights'. In: Franklin, B. (ed) *The Handbook of Children's Rights. Comparative Policy and Practice*, 201–214. Routledge.

Essen, J., Lambert, L. & Head, J. (1976) 'School Attainment of Children Who Have Been in Care'. *Child Care, Health and Development*, 2: 339–351.

Fanshel, D. & Shinn, E. (1978) *Children in Foster Care*. New York: Columbia University Press.

Farmer, E. & Parker, R. (1991) *Trials and Tribulations*. HMSO.

Fleeman, A.M.F. (1984) 'From Special to Secondary School for Children with Learning Difficulties'. *Special Education, Forward Trends*, 11(3).

Fletcher, B. (1993) *Not Just a Name: The Views of Young People in Foster and Residential Care*. National Consumer Council/Who Cares? Trust.

Fletcher, B. (1995) 'Looked After Pupils' Experience of Education and Exclusion from School'. In: Blyth, E. & Hollingsworth, S. (eds) *The Prevention and Management of Exclusion from School: An Inter-agency Conference*. Centre for Education Welfare Studies, University of Huddersfield.

Fletcher, B. (1996) *Who Cares About Education?* Who Cares? Trust.

Fletcher, B. (1998) Paper to Seminar 'Achieving Success in the Education of Looked After Children' February 1998, University of Dundee and BAAF.

Fletcher-Campbell, F. (1990) 'In Care? In School?' *Children & Society*, 4(4): 365–373.

Fletcher-Campbell, F. (1997) *The Education of Children who are Looked After*. Slough: National Foundation for Educational Research.

Fletcher-Campbell, F. (1998) 'Progress or Procrastination'. *Children & Society*, 12(1).

Fletcher-Campbell, F. & Hall, C. (1990) *Changing Schools? Changing People? The Education of Children in Care*. Slough: National Foundation for Educational Research.

Fonagy, P., Steele, H., Higgitt, A. & Target, M. (1994) 'The Theory and Practice of Resilience'. *Journal of Child Psychology*, 35(2): 231–257.

Francis, J. (1997) 'Learning to Collaborate: Developing a Joint Approach to the Education of Looked After Children'. A Centre Piece Paper. Glasgow: Centre for Residential Child Care.

Francis, J. & Thomson, G. (1996) *Improving the Educational Experience of Children in Care*. New Waverley Paper. Department of Social Work, University of Edinburgh.

Francis, J. Thomson, G. & Mills, S. (1995) *The Quality of the Educational Experience of Children in Care: A Report to Lothian Regional Council Departments of Social Work and Education*. University of Edinburgh.

Freeman, I., Morrison, A., Lockhart, F. & Swanson, M. (1996) 'Consulting Service Users: The Views of Young People'. In: Hill, M. & Aldgate, J. (eds) *Child Welfare Services*. Jessica Kingsley.

Frier, B. (1994) 'Learning and Teaching'. In: Munn, P (ed) *Schooling with Care*. Edinburgh: Scottish Office.

Frones, I. (1995) *Among Peers*. Oslo: Scandinavian University Press.

Fulcher, G. (1989) *Disabling Policies? A Comparative Approach to Education Policy and Disability*. The Falmer Press.

Gallagher, R. (1996) *Confidentiality in Schools.* Unpublished report. Glasgow: Scottish Child Law Centre.

Garmezy, N. (1985) 'Stress-Resistant Children: The Search for Protective Factors'. In: Stevenson, J.E. (ed) *Recent Research in Developmental Psychopathology.* Pergamon.

Garnett, L. (1992) *Leaving Care and After: A Follow-up Study to the Placement Outcomes Project.* National Childrens Bureau.

Gibbons, J., Gallagher, B., Bell, C. & Gordon, D. (1995) *Development After Physical Abuse in Childhood.* HMSO.

Gilligan, R. (1997) 'Beyond Permanence? The Importance of Resilience in Child Placement Practice and Planning'. *Adoption and Fostering,* 20(2).

Gilligan, R. (1998) 'The Importance of Schools and Teachers in Child Welfare'. *Child and Family Social Work,* 3(1).

Goldson, B. (1997) '"Childhood": An Introduction to Historical and Theoretical Analysis'. In: Scraton, P. (ed) *'Childhood' in Crisis.* UCL Press.

Grimshaw, R. & Berridge, D. (1994) *Educating Disruptive Children.* National Children's Bureau.

Hadley, R. & Wilkinson, H. (1995) 'Integration and Its Future: A Case Study of Primary Education and Physical Disability'. *Disability & Society,* 10(3): 309–323.

Harvey, J. (1992) 'A Postal Survey of Heads of Residential Child Care Units in Scotland'. In: *The Review of Residential Child care in Scotland: Three Supporting Research Studies.* Edinburgh: Scottish Office Central Research Unit.

Hayden, C. (1997) *Children Excluded from Primary School: Debates, Evidence, Responses.* Buckingham: Open University Press.

Haydon, D. (1997) '"Crisis" in the Classroom'. In: Scraton, P (ed) 'Childhood' in Crisis. UCL Press

Hazel, N. (1981) *A Bridge to Independence.* Oxford: Blackwell.

Heath, A., Colton, M. & Aldgate, J. (1994) 'Failure to Escape: A Longitudinal Study of Foster Children's Educational Attainment'. *British Journal of Social Work,* 24: 241–260.

Henderson, D. (1998) 'Targets Proposed for Pupils in Care'. *Times Educational Supplement Scotland* 25/9/98.

Her Majesty's Inspectorate (1990) *Choosing with Care: A report by Her Majesty's Inspectors of Schools on the Provision for Pupils with Behavioural, Emotional and Social Difficulties.* Edinburgh: Scottish Office Education Department.

Herrenkohl, E. C., Herrenkohl, R. C. & Egolf, M. A. (1994) 'Resilient Early School-Age Children from Maltreating Homes: Outcomes in Late Adolescence'. *American Journal of Orthopsychiatry,* 64(2): 301–309.

Hill, M. (1995) 'Young People's Views of Social Work and Care Services'. *Child Care in Practice,* 2(1): 49–59.

Hill, M., Nutter, R., Giltinan, D., Hudson, J. & Galaway, B. (1993) 'A Comparative Survey of Specialist Fostering Schemes in the UK and North America'. *Adoption & Fostering,* 17(2): 17–22.

Hill, M. & Tisdall, K. (1997) *Children & Society*. Harlow: Longman.

Hill, M, Triseliotis, J & Borland, M (1995) 'Social Work Services for Teenagers'. In: Hill, M., Kirk, R. & Part, D. (ed) *Supporting Families*. Edinburgh: HMSO.

Hill, M., Triseliotis, J., Borland, M. & Lambert, L. (1996) 'Fostering Adolescents in Britain: Outcomes and Processes'. *Community Alternatives*, 8(1): 77–94.

House of Commons (1984) *Children in Care*. Second Report from the Social Services Committee. HMSO.

Howe, C. (1997) *Gender and Classroom Interaction: A Research Review*. Edinburgh: The Scottish Council for Research in Education.

Howe, D. (1996) *Attachment Theory and Child and Family Social Work*. Aldershot: Avebury.

Howe, T. (1995) 'Former Pupils' Reflections on Residential Special Provision'. In: Lloyd-Smith, M. & Davies, J. (eds) *On the Margins: The Educational Experiences of 'Problem' Pupils*. Stoke on Trent: Trentham Books.

Humberside County Council (1995) *The Educational Attainments and Destinations of Young People Looked After by Humberside County Council*. Humberside County Council.

Jackson, B. & Marsden, D. (1966) *Education and the Working Class*. Middlesex: Penguin.

Jackson, S. (1987) *The Education of Children in Care*. Bristol Paper in Applied Social Studies. University of Bristol.

Jackson, S. (1989) 'The Education of Children in Care'. In: Kahan, B. (ed) *Child Care: Research, Policy and Practice*. Hodder and Stoughton.

Jackson, S. (1994) 'Education on Residential Child Care'. *Oxford Review of Education*, 20(3): 267–279.

Jackson, S. (1995) 'Education in Care: Not Somebody Else's Problem'. *British Association of Social Workers Newsletter*, November, 12–13.

Jackson, S. (1995) *Transforming Lives: The Crucial Role of Education for Young People in the Care System*. First Tory Laughland Memorial Lecture. Who Cares? Trust.

James, A. & Prout, A. (1997) *Constructing and Reconstructing Childhood*. Falmer Press.

Jenks, C. (1996) *Childhood*. Routledge.

Kahan, B. (1979) *Growing Up in Care*. Oxford: Blackwell.

Kendrick, A. (1995a) *Residential Care in the Integration of Child Care Services*. Research Findings 5. Edinburgh: Scottish Office Central Research Unit.

Kendrick, A. (1995b) 'The Integration of Child Care Services in Scotland'. *Children & Youth Services Review*, 17(5/6): 619–636.

Kendrick, A. (1995c) 'Supporting Families through Interagency Work: Youth Strategies in Scotland'. In: Hill, M., Kirk, R. & Part, D. (eds) *Supporting Families*. Edinburgh: HMSO.

Kendrick, A. (1997) 'Safeguarding Children Living Away from Home from Abuse: A Literature Review'. In: Kent, R. *Children's Safeguards Review*. Edinburgh: The Stationery Office. (Summarised in Kendrick, A. *Bullying and Peer Abuse in Residential Child Care*. Centre for Residential Child Care, Strathclyde University.

Kendrick, A., Fraser, S., Borland, M. & Harvey, J. (1992) *The Review of Residential Child Care in Scotland: Three Supporting Research Studies*. Edinburgh: Scottish Office Central Research Unit.

Kendrick, A., Simpson, M. & Mapstone, E. (1996) *Getting it Together: Changing Services for Children and Young People in Difficulty*. York: Joseph Rowntree Foundation.

Kent, R. (1997) *Children's Safeguards Review*. Edinburgh: The Stationery Office.

[Kilbrandon Report]. Scottish Home and Health Department and the Scottish Education Department (1964) *Children and Young Persons Scotland*. Report to the Committee Appointed by the Secretary of State for Scotland. Presented to Parliament April 1964. Cm 2306. Edinburgh: HMSO.

Knapp, M., Bryson, D., & Lewis, J. (1985) *The Objectives of Child Care and their Attainment Over a Twelve Month Period for a Cohort of New Admissions*. The Suffolk Cohort Study, Discussion Paper, 373. PSSRU. Canterbury: University of Kent.

Lambert, L., Essen, J. & Head, J. (1977) 'Variations in Behaviour Ratings of Children Who Have Been in Care'. *Journal of Child Psychology*, 18: 335–346.

Laybourn, A., Brown, J. & Hill, M. (1996) *Hurting on the Inside*. Aldershot: Avebury.

Levy, A. & Kahan, B. (1991) *The Pindown Experience and the Protection of Children: Report of the Staffordshire Child Care Inquiry*. Staffordshire County Council.

Little, V. & Tomlinson, J. (1993) 'Education: Thirty Years of Change – for Better or for Worse?'. In: Pugh, G. (ed) *Thirty Years of Change for Children*. National Children's Bureau.

Lockhart, F. *et al* (1996) *Strathclyde Regional Council Social Work Department School/ Training/ Employment Survey*. Unpublished.

Lorenz, W. (1994) *Social Work in a Changing Europe*. Routledge.

Loughran, F., Parker, R. & Gordon, D. (1992) *Children with Disabilities in Communal Establishments: A Further Analysis and Interpretation of the OPCS Investigation*. Department of Social Policy and Social Planning, University of Bristol.

Lücker-Babel, M. (1995) 'The Right of the Child to Express Views and to be Heard: An Attempt to Interpret Article 12 of the UN Convention on the Rights of the Child'. *The International Journal of Children's Rights*, 3: 391–404.

Maginnis, E. (1993) *An Inter-Agency Response to Children with Special Needs – The Lothian Experience – A Scottish Perspective*. Paper presented at conference: 'Exclusions from Schools: Bridging the Gap between Policy and Practice' organised by the National Children's Bureau, 13 July, National Children's Bureau.

Mahood, L. (1995) *Policing Gender, Class and Family: Britain 1850–1940*. UCL Press.

Marshall, K. (1997) *Children's Rights in the Balance. Reconciling Views and Interests*. Edinburgh: The Stationery Office.

Maughan, B. (1988) 'School Experiences as Risk/Protective Factors'. In: Rutter, M. (ed) *Studies of Psychosocial Risk: The Power of Longitudinal Data.* Cambridge University Press.

McAuley, C. (1996) 'Children's Perspectives on Long-term Foster Care'. In: Hill, M. & Aldgate, J. (eds) *Child Welfare Services.* Jessica Kingsley.

McAuley, C. (1996) *Children in Long Term Foster Care.* Aldershot: Avebury.

McCann, A. (1997) 'Private Cash for Council Schools'. *The Scotsman,* 5.12.97.

McColm, E. (1998) 'Anger As Schools Get the Axe'. *The Scotsman,* 18.2.98.

McCullogh, D. (1991) *Developing a Strategy: A Study of School Liaison Groups in Central Region.* Glasgow: Jordanhill College.

McDonnel, P. & Aldgate, J. (1984) 'Review Procedures of Children in Care'. *Adoption and Fostering,* 8(2).

McKay, B. (1994) 'Interagency Approaches'. In: Munn, P. (ed) *Schooling with Care.* Edinburgh: Scottish Office.

McLean, A. (1994) 'Staff Development'. In: Munn, P. (ed) *Schooling with Care.* Edinburgh: Scottish Office.

McParlin, P. (1996a) *Children from a Promised Land.* Leeds: First Key.

McParlin, P. (1996b) *It's Never too Late.* Leeds: First Key.

McParlin, P. (1996c) *Careers for those Leaving Care.* Leeds: First Key.

McParlin, P. (1996d) *Born to Fail (In tribute to Fred Fever).* Leeds: First Key.

McParlin, P. (1996e) *The Primary Education of Children Looked After (In care).* Leeds: First Key.

Measor, L. & Sykes, P. (1992) *Gender and Schools.* Cassell.

Mellor, A. (1997) *Bullying at School: Advice for Families.* Edinburgh: SCRE.

Menmuir, R. (1994) 'Involving Residential Social Workers and Foster Carers in Reading with Young People in their Care: The PRAISE Reading Project'. *Oxford Review of Education,* 20(3).

Midwinter, A. & McGarvey, N. (1994) 'The Restructuring of Scotland's Education Authorities: Does Size Matter?' *Scottish Educational Review,* 26(2): 110–117.

Millham, S., Bullock, R., Hosie, K. & Haak, M. (1986) *Lost in Care.* Aldershot: Gower.

Mitchell, A. (1985) *Children in the Middle.* Tavistock.

Mitchell, D. (1997) 'Children's Services Go Over to Charities'. *Community Care,* 20–26 February.

Munn, P. (1994) (ed) *Schooling with Care.* Edinburgh: Scottish Office.

National Foster Care Association (1996) *Education: A Guide for Foster Carers.* Signposts in Foster Care. NFCA.

Nelson, D. (1998) 'Education Battle to Save League Tables'. *The Observer,* 1.3.98.

Office for Standards in Education and Social Services Inspectorate (Ofsted) (1995) *The Education of Children who are Looked-After by local Authorities.* Ofsted/ SSI.

Olsen, F. (1992) 'Social Legislation. Sex Bias in International Law: The UN Convention on the Rights of the Child'. *Indian J. of Social Work* 53(3): 491–516.

Osborn, A. & St Claire, L. (1987) 'The Ability and Behaviour of Children who have been in Care or Separated from their Parents'. *Early Child Development and Care*, 28(3): 187–354.

Packman, J., Randall, J. & Jacques, N. (1986) *Who Needs Care?* Oxford: Blackwell.

Page, R. & Clark, G. (1977) *Who Cares? Young People in Care Speak Out.* National Children's Bureau.

Parker, R.A. (1980) *Caring for Separated Children.* MacMillan.

Parker, R.A. (1988) 'Residential Care for Children'. In: Sinclair, I. (ed) *Residential Care: The Research Reviewed.* HMSO.

Parker, R., Ward, H., Jackson, S., Aldgate, J. & Wedge, P. (1991) *Assessing Outcomes in Child Care.* HMSO.

Parson, C. (1996) 'Permanent Exclusions from School in England in the 1990s: Trends, Causes and Responses'. *Children & Society*, 10(3): 177–186.

Parton, N. (1985) *The Politics of Child Abuse.* Macmillan.

Parton, N. (1991) *Governing the Family.* Macmillan.

Phillips, M. & Worlock, D. (1996) 'A Big Step Forward for Children and Foster Carers: Implementing the Looked After Children System in RBKC'. *Adoption & Fostering*, 20(4).

Pickup, M. (1987) *A Critical Analysis of a Research Study by A.M.F. Fleeman.* MEd Thesis, University of Exeter.

Pilling, D. (1990) *Escape from Disadvantage.* Falmer.

Pilling, D. (1992) 'Escaping from a Bad Start'. In: Tizard, B. & Varma, V. (eds) *Vulnerability and Resilience in Human Development.* Jessica Kingsley.

Quinton, D., Rushton, A., Dance, C. & Mayes, D. (1996) *Establishing Permanent Placements in Middle Childhood.* Maudsley Adoption and Fostering Study, Report to Department of Health.

Quinton, D. & Rutter, M. (1988) *Parenting Breakdown.* Aldershot: Avebury.

Qvortrop, J., Bardy, M., Sgritta, G. & Wintersberger, H. (eds) (1994) *Childhood Matters.* Aldershot: Avebury.

Ramsey, D. (1995) Survey of the Characteristics of Children Admitted to Physical Care, Fife (unpublished).

Rea-Price, J. & Pugh (1996) *Championing Children.* National Children's Bureau/ Manchester City Council.

Riddell, S. (1996) 'Theorising Special Educational Needs in a Changing Political Climate'. In: Barton, L. (ed) *Disability and Society. Emerging Issues and Insights*, 83–106. Longman.

Rigby, K. (1996) *Bullying in Schools.* Jessica Kingsley.

Robbins, D. (1990) *Child Care Policy: Putting it in Writing.* HMSO.

Romans, S., Martin, J., Anderson, J., O'Shea, M. & Mullen, P. (1995) 'Factors that Mediate Between Child Sexual Abuse and Adult Psychological Outcome'. *Psychological Medicine*, 25: 127–142.

Rowe, J. & Lambert, L. (1973) *Children Who Wait.* British Agencies for Adoption and Fostering (BAAF).

Rutter, M. (1985) 'Resilience in the Face of Adversity'. *British Journal of Psychiatry*, 147: 598–611.

Rutter, M. (ed) (1988) *Studies of Psychosocial Risk: The Power of Longitudinal Data.* Cambridge University Press.

Rutter, M., Quinton, D. & Hill, J. (1991) 'Adult Outcomes of Institution-reared Children: Males and Females Compared'. In: Robbins, L. & Rutter, M. (eds) *Straight and Deviant Pathways from Childhood to Adulthood.* Cambridge University Press.

Rutter, M. & Rutter, M. (1993) *Developing Minds.* Harmondsworth: Penguin.

Rutter, M., Tizard, J. & Whitmore, K. (eds) (1970) *Education, Health and Behaviour.* Longman.

Sachdev, D. & Taylor, H. (1996) *The Findings of a Survey of the Educational Position of Children in Care in the South and East Belfast Trust.* Barnardo's.

Saddington, A. (1998) 'In My Experience'. *Who Cares?* 8.

Sandiford, P. (1996) *Improving Educational Opportunities for Looked After Young People: A Good Practice Guide for Teachers.* National Children's Bureau.

SCRE (1992) *Action Against Bullying: The First SCRE Anti-Bullying Pack.* Edinburgh: SCRE.

SCRE (1993) *Supporting Schools Against Bullying: The Second SCRE Anti-Bullying Pack.* Edinburgh: SCRE.

Scottish Office (1994a) *Working Together: The Scottish Office, Volunteers and Voluntary Organisations.* Edinburgh: The Scottish Office.

Scottish Office (1994b) *Teaching with Care,* Video. Scottish Office Education and Industry Department & Quality in Education Centre, University of Strathclyde.

Scottish Office (1996a) *Services for Children 1995.* Statistical Bulletin, Social Work Series, No SWK/SC/1996/5. Edinburgh: The Scottish Office.

Scottish Office (1996b) *Children in Care or under Supervision 1992 and 1993.* Statistical Bulletin, Social Work Series, No SWK/CC/1996/15. Edinburgh: The Scottish Office.

Scottish Office (1996c) *Children and Young Persons with Special Educational Needs.* SOEID Circular 4/96. Edinburgh: The Scottish Office.

Scottish Office (1996d) *Provision for Pupils with Special Educational Needs, 1993 and 1995.* Statistical Bulletin, Education Series, Edn/D2/1996/11. Edinburgh: The Scottish Office.

Scottish Office (1997a) *A Curriculum Framework for Children in their Pre School Year.* Edinburgh: The Scottish Office.

Scottish Office (1997b) *Achieving Success in S1/S2: A Report on the review of provision in S1/S2 by HM Inspectors of Schools.* Edinburgh: HMSO.

Scottish Office (1997c) *Education in Early Childhood: the pre-school years.* Consultation Paper. http://www.scotland.gov.uk/library/documents/internet.htm.

Scottish Office (1997-98) The Scottish Office Education and Industry Department published reports by HM Inspectors of Schools. Edinburgh: Scottish Office.

Scottish Office (1998a) *New Commission to Forge Future Relations between Central and Local Government.* News Release 23.1.98. http://www.scottish-devolution.org.uk/frame.htm.

Scottish Office (1998b) *Targets to Raise Standards in Scottish Schools.* News Release 4.3.98. http://www.scotland.gov.uk/news/releas98/pr0423/htm.

Scottish Office (1998c) *Social Exclusion in Scotland: A Consultation Paper.* Edinburgh: The Stationery Office. http://www.scotland. gov.uk/library/documents1/socesucl.htm.

Scottish Office (1998d) *Guidance on Issues Concerning Exclusion from School.* SOEID Circular 2/98. Edinburgh: Scottish Office.

Scottish Office (1998e) *Parents as Partners: Enhancing the Role of Parents in School Education.* A Discussion Paper. Edinburgh: Scottish Office.

Scraton, P. (1997) 'Whose "Childhood"? What "Crisis"?' In: Scraton, P. (ed) *'Childhood' in Crisis.* UCL Press.

Shaw, M. & Hipgrave, T. (1983) *Specialist Fostering.* Batsford.

Silva-Wayne, S. (1995) 'Contributions to Resilience in Children and Youth: What Successful Child Welfare Graduates Say'. In: Hudson, J. & Galaway, B. (eds) *Child Welfare in Canada: Research and Policy Implications.* Toronto: Thompson Educational Publishing.

Sinclair, R., Garnett, L. & Berridge, D. (1995) *Social Work and Assessment with Adolescents.* National Children's Bureau.

Sinclair, R., Grimshaw, R. & Garnett, L. (1994) 'The Education of Children in Need: The Impact of the Education Reform Act 1988, The Education Act 1993 and the Children Act 1989'. *Oxford Review of Education,* 20(3): 281–292.

[The Skinner Report]. Scottish Office (1992) *Another Kind of Home: Review of Residential Child Care in Scotland.* Edinburgh: HMSO.

Smith, P.K. & Sharp, S. (eds) (1994) *School Bullying: Insights and Perspectives.* Routledge.

Social Services Inspectorate (SSI) (1994) *Services to Disabled Children and Their Families.* Report of the National Inspection of Services to Disabled Children and their Families, January 1994. HMSO.

Social Services Inspectorate (SSI) (1997) *Responding to Families in Need: Inspection of Assessment, Planning and Decision-making in Family Support Services.* Wetherby: Department of Health.

Social Work Services Group (SWSG) (1993) *Scotland's Children: Proposals for Child Care Policy and Law.* Cm 2286. Edinburgh: HMSO.

Social Work Service Group (SWSG) (1997a) *Scotland's Children. The Children (Scotland) Act 1995 Regulations and Guidance, Volume 1: Support and Protection for Children and their Families.* Edinburgh: The Stationery Office.

Social Work Service Group (SWSG) (1997b) *Scotland's Children. The Children (Scotland) Act 1995 Regulations and Guidance, 2: Children Looked After by Local Authorities.* Edinburgh: The Stationery Office.

Social Work Service Group (SWSG) (1997c) *Scotland's Children. The Children (Scotland) Act 1995 Regulations and Guidance, 3: Adoption and Parental Responsibilities Orders.* Edinburgh: The Stationery Office.

Social Work Services Inspectorate (1996) *A Secure Remedy.* Edinburgh: SWSI.

Sparks, I. (1998) 'The Ritz Would be Cheaper by Half'. *The Guardian*, 15.4.98.

Stein, M. (1994) 'Leaving Care, Education and Career Trajectories'. *Oxford Review of Education*, 20(3).

Stein, M. & Carey, K. (1986) *Leaving Care*. Oxford: Basil Blackwell.

Stewart, F. (1996) *The Health of Young People in Care*. Dissertation for MPhil in Child Studies, University of Glasgow.

Strathclyde Regional Council (1988) *Young People in Trouble*. Glasgow: SRC.

Sutton, P. (1995) *Crossing the Boundaries: A Discussion of Children's Services Plans*. National Children's Bureau.

Sylva, K. (1994) 'School Influences on Children's Development'. *Journal of Child Psychology and Psychiatry*, 35(1): 135–172.

Thoburn, J., Lewis, A. & Shemmings, D. (1995) *Paternalism or Partnership? Family Involvement in the Child Protection Process*. HMSO.

Thoburn, J., Murdoch, A. & O'Brien, A. (1986) *Permanence in Child Care*. Blackwell.

Tisdall, K. (1996) 'From the Social Work (Scotland) Act 1968 to the Children (Scotland) Act 1995: Pressures for change'. In: Hill, M. & Aldgate, J. (eds) *Child Welfare Services*. Jessica Kingsley.

Tisdall, K. (1997) *Children (Scotland) Act 1995: Developing Policy and Law for Scotland's Children*. Edinburgh: The Stationery Office.

Tizard, B. (1977) *Adoption: A Second Chance*. Open Books.

Triseliotis, J., Borland, M. & Hill, M. (1998a) *Fostering Good Relations: A Study of Foster Care and Foster Carers in Scotland*. Edinburgh: Scottish Office, CRU.

Triseliotis, J., Borland, M. & Hill, M. (1998b) *The Structure, Organisation and Delivery of Fostering Services in Scotland*. Report to Social Work Services Group. Edinburgh: The Scottish Office.

Triseliotis, J., Borland, M., Hill, M. & Lambert, L. (1995) *Teenagers and the Social Work Services*. HMSO.

Triseliotis, J. & Russell, J. (1984) *Hard to Place*. Heineman.

Tulips, J., Hart, E.K. & Flynn, B. (1988) 'Following an Antique Drum: Some Indices of the Schooling Experience of Children in Care'. In: Scottish Education Department (1989) *New Demands and New Responses: A Comparative Evaluation of Service Delivery. Professional Development Initiatives 1988–89*. Edinburgh: SED / Regional Psychological Services.

United Nations Educational, Scientific and Cultural Organisation (UNESCO) & The Ministry of Education and Science, Spain (1994) *The Salamanca Declaration and Framework for Action on Special Needs Education*. New York: UNESCO.

Utting, W. (1991) *Children in the Public Care: A Review of Residential Child Care*. HMSO.

Utting, W. (1997) *People Like Us: The Report of the Review of the Safeguards for Children Living Away from Home*. The Stationery Office.

Van Gendt, R. (1996) *The International Resilience Project*. Ghent: Bernard van Leer Foundation.

Veerman, P.E. (1992) *The Rights of the Child and the Changing Image of Childhood.* Dordrecht: Martinus Nijhoff.

Walker, T. (1994) 'Educating Children in the Public Care: A Strategic Approach'. *Oxford Review of Education*, 20(3): 329–47.

Ward, H. (ed) (1995) *Looking After Children: Research into Practice.* HMSO.

[Warnock Report]. Committee of Enquiry into the Education of Handicapped Children and Young People (1978) *Special Educational Needs.* Cmnd. 7212. HMSO.

Werner, E.E. & Smith, R.S. (1992) *Overcoming the Odds.* Ithaca: Cornell University Press.

Wheelaghan, S., Hill, M., Borland, M. & Lambert, L. (1998) *Evaluation of 'Looked After Children' (LAC) Implementation in Scotland.* Report to Scottish Office (forthcoming).

Who Cares? Scotland (1998) Young people's presentation to Seminar 'Achieving Success in the Education of Looked After Children', February 1998. University of Dundee and BAAF.

Who Cares? Trust (1996) *The Education of Children who are Looked After by Local Authorities: A Guide for School Governors.* Who Cares? Trust.

Willms, J.D. (1997) *Parental Choice and Education Policy.* CES Briefing 12. Edinburgh: Centre for Educational Sociology, Edinburgh University.

Index

Aberlour Child Care Trust 10
abuse 29, 38, 113
'accommodated' children 26
accountability 115, 117
admissions, characteristics of 26
adoption 5, 72
   and educational attainment 41–2
Adoption (Scotland) Act (1978) 5
adulthood, transition to 44–6
after-care 23
after-school care 19
age, looked after children 26–8
Aldgate, Jane, *The Educational Progress of Children in Foster Care* 3, 121–2
alternative education programmes 50, 51
alternative educational provision 35, 64–9
assessment 6, 20, 24
assessment and action records 72–3
assessment centres 27, 64
Assisted Places Scheme 11
attitudes
   new, towards children 114–15
   of teachers and social workers 104–5
Ayre, Patrick, *Hello – Is Anybody Listening?* 3, 123–6

Barrett, David, *Hello – Is Anybody Listening?* 3, 123–6
behaviour problems at school 34–5
Berridge, David, *Hello – Is Anybody Listening?* 3, 123–6
birth parents, involving 81–2
Brodie, Isabelle, *Hello – Is Anybody Listening?* 3, 123–6
bullying 54, 57, 58, 84, 119

care and education
   close links 31, 71–92
   institutions involved 100
care careers 51–2
care continuum, educational continuity in 77–8

care experience, categories of and outcomes 45–6
care planning 14, 106
   need for synchronisation with education 107
care system, impact on education 71–92
careers service 10
carers
   attachment to 71–2
   educational background of 89, 91
   need for training 110
   roles and effective contact with the school 79–81, 129
centralisation 9
chief social work officer 6
child, or children 15; *see also* individual children
child crime 115
Child Health and Education Study 41–2
child-care managers 103
child-care policy and practice, developments in 71–3
child-care reviews 11, 14, 106–7
'child-proofing' policy 21
childhood, sociology of 114
childminding 6
children, interaction with adults 119
Children Act (1989) 3, 5–6, 12, 19
children in care *see* looked after children
children living away from home *see* looked after children
children in need 15, 16–19, 25
   defined 16, 18–19
   legislation 23–4
children in public care *see* looked after children
Children (Scotland) Act (1995) 1, 3, 5, 11, 13, 14–15, 18, 19, 72, 81, 112
Children's Hearing System, Scotland 2, 14, 93
children's homes
   closure 34
   educational arrangements for 50, 53
   educational environment in 125

see also residential units
Children's Reporters 9
children's rights 8, 11, 12–13, 15–16
    concerns about 114–15
children's rights officers 12
Children's Services Plans 19, 21, 93, 94,
    116
Citizen's Charters 10
class *see* social class
client groups, 'unpopular' 8
collaboration
    between social work and education 14,
        93–108
    in relation to individual children 106
    structures for 101–5
college packages, special 35
Colton, Matthew, *Educational Progress of
    Children in Foster Care* 3, 121–2
commitment 79
'community care' 6
community councils 8
compensatory experience 31–2
competition 10–12
compulsory admissions to schools 32
compulsory orders 26, 28
confidentiality in school 105, 109
consumerism 10–12, 115
continuity 76–8
Convention of Scottish Local
    Authorities (CoSLA) 7
coping skills, acquisition of 37–8
corporate parenting 116–17
    and links with schools 78–83
counselling, pre-learning 119
curricula 9

day-care 6, 10, 19
    intermediate treatment 35
day-units, special 35, 64
decentralisation 7–8
deinstitutionalisation and inclusion 13–14
disabilities
    children with 6, 13–14, 20, 24, 25
    looked after children with 28, 35
disability, defined 24
Disability Discrimination Act (1995) 6, 14

Disabled Persons (Services,
    Consultation and Representation) Act
    (1986) 6, 20
disadvantage, social 30, 41
'disaffected' children 29
discipline 115
    promoting school 21
discontinuity 76–8, 119
'drifting' children 71–2
Dumfries and Galloway 98

early educational intervention 21, 42
early years services 21
education and care
    close links 31
    institutions involved 100
    collaboration with social work
        93–108
    impact of care system on 71–92
    the importance of 73–4, 117
    of looked after children 2, 127–9
    and residential care 83–90, 123–6,
        131–2
    role in promoting resilience 36–9
education authorities, duties of 5, 17
*Education of Children being Looked After
    by Local Authorities*, England and
    Wales (1994) 48–9
Education (Scotland) Act (1980) 5, 10, 18
education support services, looked after
    children 102–3, 128
education/care careers 51–2
educational arrangements 50–6
educational attainment 36, 40–6, 117
    able children 35–6, 132
    or emotional well-being 71
    in foster care 42–3, 91
    Humberside study 43–4
    leaving-care studies 44–6
    national cohort studies 40–2
    Ofsted/SSI inspection 43
educational disadvantage 109–11
educational experience, while away
    from home 47–70, 129–32
educational plans 96
educational policy 2, 47–50

educational progress 100, 121–3
educational provision
    alternative 35
    in secure accommodation 68–9
educational psychologists 103
emergency orders 26
emotional well-being, or educational
    attainment 59, 71
employment experiences 44, 45
England and Wales 2, 18–19, 48–9
    policy and practice 94–5
Equal Chances project 94–5, 98–9, 117
European Convention on Human
    Rights (ECHR) 13
exclusion
    alternatives to school 21
    explanations of 15, 54–6
    levels of 52–4
    national guidance on 55
    and parenting 82–3
    social 21, 117
expectations, of looked after children
    74–5
experiences, understanding children's 119

Falkirk Council 10
families, on income support 30
family placement, long-term 72
fathers, unmarried 16
Fife Council, social strategies 6
Fife in-house study 32, 34
Fletcher-Campbell, Felicity,
    Changing School? Changing People? 3,
        126–7
    The Education of Children who are
        Looked After 3, 127–9
foster care 13, 90–2
    educational attainment in 42–3, 121–3
    educational environment in 90–2
    number of families in Scotland 26
    recommendations for 112
foster carers
    interest and commitment 79
    responsibilities of 81
    training for 91
fostering, 'professional' or 'specialist' 27

Francis, Joe, The Quality of the
    Educational Experience of Children in
    Care 3, 129–31
friendships 119
funding problems 104, 116
further education colleges 10
Future Needs Assessments (FNAs) 17, 20

gate-keeping procedures 32, 33
Glasgow Council 10
good practice 47–50
grant-maintained schools see opting out
    schools
grounds of referral 28–9
guidance 47–50

Hall, Chris, Changing School? Changing
    People? 3, 126–7
head teachers, attitudes to school
    exclusion 55
Health, Department of, 'research into
    practice' child-care series 2
health boards 7
health needs 84
Heath, Anthony, The Educational
    Progress of Children in Foster Care 3,
    121–2
Henderson, Bernadette, Hello – Is
    Anybody Listening? 3, 123–6
Her Majesty's Inspectorate of Schools
    (HMI) 3
    responsibilities 28
Higher Still 9
holiday care 19
home supervision 1, 13
home tutors 35
home-school agreements 16
homework, facilities in residential units
    for 85–6
hospitals 27
housing 30
Humberside Study 43–4

ideologies, evolving 6–14, 114
inclusion 99, 115–16
    and deinstitutionalisation 13–14
independent schools 11

individual children
  collaboration in relation to 106
  recommendations for 112, 113
institutional policy 111–12
integration into school 32, 65, 99
inter-agency liaison group, school-
  based 103–4
inter-professional processes 119–20
intervention, levels and timing of 21, 42,
  105
Inverclyde Children's Units Support
  Project 96–8

Jackson, Sonia, *Succeeding in Care –
  Residential Care and Education* 3, 131–2
Joint Boards 6
Joint Committees 6
joint parenting 16
joint working 49, 101
  barriers to 104–5
  developing 93–108
joint youth strategies 101–2, 103

Kilbrandon report (1964) 93

Labour Government 21
learning difficulty 16–17
learning projects, out-of-school-hours 21
leaving-care studies, educational
  attainment 44–6
legislation 5–6
  children in need 23–4
  linkages and comparisons 14–20
  'looked after children' 22–3
link teachers 95–6, 97–8, 103
local authorities
  complaints procedures 10
  corporate definition of 14, 15
  duties of consultation with parents 81
  duties to looked after children 22, 30,
    112
  duty to meet children's welfare 5
  as enabling authorities 9
  as parents *see* corporate parenting
  recommendations for 111
  responsibilities of 1, 14
  structural changes 6–7

local authority homes 27
Local Government etc (Scotland) Act
  (1994) 6, 8
longitudinal research 118–19
looked after children 25–30
  age and type of placement 26–8
  characteristics 30
  definition 18
  with disabilities 28, 35
  education support services 102–3
  educational attainment 40–6
  educational experience 47–70,
    129–32
  educational situation of 109–11, 127–9
  expectations of 74–5
  legal status 26
  legislation on 22–3
  length of time in care 26
  and mainstream schools 61–3
  meaning of term 1
  reasons for care 28–9
  in specialist educational provision 65–6
Looking After Children 72–3, 74, 107, 108

mainstream schools
  and looked after young people 61–3
  views of young people 56–61
marginalisation 4, 54
marketisation 10–12
Mental Health (Scotland) Act (1984) 24
Midlothian 98
Mills, Sue, *The Quality of the Educational
  Experience of Children in Care* 3, 129–31
Modern Apprenticeships 9
Moray Council 9

National Child Development Study 40–
  1, 45
National Childcare Strategy 21
National Health Service and
  Community Care Act (1990) 6
national policy 111
NCH Action for Children Scotland 9
need
  children in *see* children in need
  definitions of 18–19
  identification of 25

needs
    educational 4
    educational and emotional 59
    health 84
neglect 29
New Deal 9, 21
non-attendance at school 28, 29, 34–5
    explanations of 54–6
    levels 52–4
    residential units and 88–9

offenders 28, 29
Ofsted 3
Ofsted/SSI report 43, 79–80, 82, 105, 106
opting out schools 5, 11, 17

parental care, lack of 28
parental choice 10, 11
parental responsibility orders 26
parenting, when children are excluded
    from school 82–3
parents
    adoptive, interest and commitment 79
    contribution to schooling 78–9
    identifying the role of 16
    responsibilities of both 116
    support for 1
    unable to cope 28, 29
    views of residential schooling 67
    see also birth parents; corporate
        parenting; foster carers; joint
        parenting
Parent's Charter 10
parents' rights 11, 15–16
partnership 99, 116–17
    with parents 84
    school-parent 21
peer-relationships 38, 119
personal interest 79
placement
    choice of 28, 106
    moves of 28, 76–7, 119, 126–7
    patterns of 50
    short-term outcomes for residential
        schools 67–8
    for teenagers 27
    type of 26–8

Plowden Report (1967) 78
police 7
    initiatives on children being home at
        a given time 115
policy
    England and Wales 94–5
    implications for 109–20
    key elements of effective 98–101
    Scotland 95–8
    see also child-care policy; educational
        policy; national policy
poverty 30
practice, implications for 109–20
PRAISE project, Salford 91–2
pre-school education 10, 118
prevention, priority to 102
primary schools, looked after children
    in 49, 61–2, 63
Private Finance Initiative 10
private sector 10
problems, precipitating entry into care 29
project evaluation 120
'protected' children 29

referral, grounds of 28–9
refuge, children who take 22
Renfrewshire, Children in Care Joint
    Support Project 98
research, implications for 109–20
research studies
    differentiation in 118
    longitudinal 118–19
    omissions in 117–20
residential care 27
    decrease in use 13
    and education 83–90, 123–6, 131–2
    evaluation of 83–5
    recommendations for 112
residential placements, aims of 27–8
residential provision, statistics on 26–7
Residential Regulations (1987) 80
residential schools 27, 33–4, 66–8
    day attendance at 35
    links with schools 80
    roles of 64
residential staff 125–6

actions in promoting education 86–7
    training/educational background 89
residential units
    educational environment of 85
    facilities for homework 85–6
    and non-attendance at school 88–9
    school-related routine in 87–8
    support services and integrated
        practice 90
    see also children's homes
resilience 69, 72
    defined 36
    factors associated with 37
    role of education in promoting 36–9
respite, regular 26
responsibility 5–24
    lack of clear guidance 110
return home, schooling on 62–3
rights see children's rights; parents'
    rights
routine, school-related in residential
    homes 87–8

safety 84
Sandiford, P. 49
school boards, representation for looked
    after children at 16
School Boards (Scotland) Act (1988) 5
school experience
    mainstream 56–61
    positive 59–61
school league tables 11, 54
school management, devolved 8, 17
school practice, principles for children
    with emotional and behavioural
    difficulties 48
school problems
    need for early recognition 33
    precipitating care away from home
        32–3
    types of 34–6
schooling
    parents' contribution to 78–9
    on return home 62–3

schools
    changes of 76–7, 126–7
    cooperation with welfare services
        110–12
    links in corporate parenting 78–83
    looked after children in 49, 61–2, 63,
        113, 129
    patterns of experience 51–2
    qualities of best 38
    recommendations for 111–12, 112–13
    roles and effective contact of carers
        with 79–81
    the significance of 31–9, 110
    as a supportive service 31–2
    whole-school approaches 47–8
    see also mainstream schools; primary
        schools; secondary schools; special
        schools
Scotland for Children Campaign 8
Scottish Children's Reporters
    Administration 9
Scottish Commission (1998) 7–8
Scottish Office
    Education and Industry Department
        (SOEID) 1, 14, 15
    Minister for Children's Issues 21
Scottish Parliament 7–8
secondary schools, looked after children
    in 49, 61–2, 63, 113
'Section 13' assessment of disabled
    children with SEN records 6, 20
secure accommodation, education in
    68–9
self-governing schools 5, 11
Self-Governing Schools etc. (Scotland)
    Act (1989) 5
service development
    England and Wales 94–5
    Scotland 95–8
sex education 60
Skill Seekers 9
Skinner Report (1992) 3, 34, 48, 78
    principles for residential child-care
        13, 83–4
social class, and parental choice 10
Social Exclusion Network 21

Social Exclusion Unit 21
social work, collaboration with education 93–108
Social Work Inspectorate (SSI) 3
social work records, on teenagers 35
Social Work (Scotland) Act (1968) 5, 14
social work services, purchasing power 9
Social Work Services Group (SWSG) 1, 3, 14, 15
   guidance 14, 16, 17–18
social workers
   attitudes and expectations 73–6, 104–5
   links with schools 80–1
   responsibilities of 81, 82
   and teachers 59
   understanding and knowledge of education 75–6
South Lanarkshire, Educational Support Service for Children in Care 95–6, 103
special educational needs (SEN) 16–19
   defined 16
   record of 17, 20
   Statements/Records 17
special needs teachers 101
special schools 27, 28
specialist educational provision 17, 64–9
   effectiveness of 64–5
   looked after children in 65–6
   types of 64
standards, educational 21
statutes see legislation
stigmatisation 25–6, 54, 66, 109
success at school 36, 37, 132
supervision orders 26, 28
support services, availability of 31–2, 90

teachers
   attitudes 104–5
   communication with birth parents 82
   guides for 48–9
   helpful behaviour from 58–9, 60–1, 68–9
   role in child-care reviews 106–7
   views of young people on 58–9
   see also head teachers; link teachers; special needs teachers

teachers' reports 32
teenagers
   placements for 27, 90
   school problems of 35
Thomson, George, The Quality of the Educational Experience of Children in Care 3, 129–31
Through-Care Services Report 96
truancy see non-attendance at school

underachievement 40–1, 43
United Nations Convention on the Rights of the Child 1, 12

'victims' of abuse 29
views of children 2, 12, 15, 119
   as consumers of a service 115
   on specialist provision 66
views of teachers, on looked after children 25, 61
views of young people 49–50, 110, 112, 114–15
   on education 60
   mainstream schools 56–61
   on teachers 58–9
'villains' 29
vocationalism 9
voluntary homes 27
voluntary organisations 7, 9
'volunteers' to come into care 28, 29
vouchers, pre-school 10, 11

Wales see England and Wales
Warnock Report (1978) 17, 78
welfare, mixed economy of 9–10
welfare services, cooperation with schools 110–12
Wenman, Helen, Hello – Is Anybody Listening? 3, 123–6
Who Cares? Trust 94, 115, 119
   book-buying scheme 87

young people in care see looked after children